DIARY of a FRENCH HERB GARDEN

DIARY of a
FRENCH HERB
GARDEN

Geraldene Holt

PAVILION

First published in Great Britain in 2002 by
PAVILION BOOKS LIMITED
64 Brewery Road
London N7 9NT
www.chrysalisbooks.co.uk

A member of **Chrysalis** Books plc

Text © Geraldene Holt 2002
Design and layout © Pavilion Books Ltd.

The moral right of the author has been asserted

Designed by David Fordham
Map illustration by Gill Tomblin

A CIP catalogue record for this book is available from the British Library

ISBN 1 86205 488 6

Set in Bernhardt Modern and Galliard
Printed in Italy by G. Canale and C.S.p.A.

2 4 6 8 10 9 7 5 3 1

This book can be ordered direct from the publisher. Please contact
the Marketing Department. But try your bookshop first.

Contents

DEDICATION

I dedicate this book to all my friends in Saint Montan

ACKNOWLEDGEMENTS

IN TELLING THIS STORY I've taken the opportunity to mention many people who contributed in various ways to the making of the garden. I am grateful to them all. I should also like to record my thanks to the mayor and councillors of Saint Montan for agreeing to my proposal. I am particularly indebted to my friends, Suzanne and Jeanette Doize, for their years of kindness and encouragement. On countless summer evenings, my husband dutifully tended the needs of thirsty plants. My daughter acts as a willing weeding assistant whenever she visits, and my mother has given the garden its sundial. I thank each one most warmly for helping the village herb garden to become a reality.

www.geraldeneholt.com

DIARY of a FRENCH HERB GARDEN

THE PROLOGUE AND GARDENING YEAR

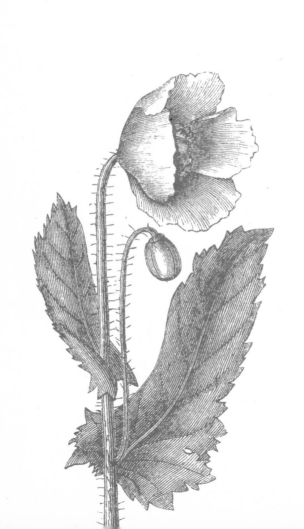

Prologue

THE ROAD TURNS OFF the *route nationale* and climbs slowly west from the wide valley of the river Rhône. Vineyards and fields of lavender unfold on either side as far as the *garrigue*-covered horizon. At the crest of the slope, you glimpse the ruined château of Saint Montan, its golden stone silhouetted against the bleak grey rocks. Suddenly, the road curves abruptly to the left and you swing down, following the wall of the cemetery, into the cluster of houses in the centre of the village.

We drove into Saint Montan for the first time almost twenty years ago, and I was immediately captivated. But we were on vacation and our destination was the nearby hamlet of Larnas, renowned for its Romanesque chapel. So we continued through the village, taking the steep, sinuous route hewn from the sheer face of the gorge, to reach our rented *gîte* on the high Ardèchois plateau in the shadow of the Dent de Rez mountain.

Since there are no shops in Larnas, the next day we returned down the gorge road to explore Saint Montan on foot. I remember how seductively sleepy the place was, with few people to be seen, though there was a *boulangerie*, a post office and a small, dark shop that appeared to sell everything from candles to espadrilles and local *charcuterie*. We bought food for a picnic lunch and sat on the big flat stones beside the tumbling river, looking up at the dilapidated residences of the medieval village.

For a few years we continued to rent a *gîte* in the Larnas *presbytère* each summer, and we made good friends in the area. We grew to love the Ardèche, one of France's least populous regions with few large towns or remnants of any aristocratic past. Much of the Ardèche is truly *la France profonde* where living has always been hard and little has changed for generations. The shallow soil and high altitude make agriculture singularly arduous, though chestnut, almond and cherry trees flourish on the terraced terrain. Goats scramble over rocky outcrops, while in the valleys the fig and the vine are often able to take hold. And, until a century ago, the leaves of the white mulberry tree provided food for the silkworms that were bred on the upper floor of almost every farmhouse.

The geography of the *département*, with a climate that varies from alpine to Mediterranean, and whose culinary contrasts

range from cooking with butter in the north to olive oil in the south, make the Ardèche almost a microcosm of France itself. Yet, aside from the grandeur of its scenery, and the superb quality of its food, it is the character of its people that I warm to most: courageous, loyal and fiercely independent. When they become your friends, you are indeed blessed. As we departed each year, we dreamed of buying our own small *gîte*, just a cottage with a strip of garden, that could become our summer home.

At last, we heard that the village postman in Saint Montan wanted to sell his house, beside the stream as you enter the village from the gorge. And so, a few months later, in the office of the local *notaire*, we became *Saint Montanais* – at least by adoption.

We began to spend more and more time in our French home. Eventually, five years ago, we packed the car with books, wedged in our three English cats, and drove south to begin a new life in the Midi. Like me, the cats took to the place from the moment they arrived.

Our little stone house is built directly into the steep hillside at the foot of the gorge. The garden is a series of long narrow terraces, and the lowest ends in a dry-stone wall which separates it from another plot, once tended by the village priest – and thus a genuine *jardin du curé* – though it had been neglected for decades.

One September day, we returned to Saint Montan to discover that the *mairie* had begun to cut down the fig trees in the *curé's* old garden. Neighbours told us that the mayor planned to construct a picnic place there for visitors to the village, and an unappealing vision of fly-blown sandwich papers and empty Orangina bottles came to mind. It was time to visit the mayor. I asked my good Larnas friend Suzanne Doize, herself a retired mayor, to accompany me.

The mayor explained that he couldn't sell me the *curé's* old garden, or even rent it to me. 'You see, the Catholic church owns the land and has leased it to us, for the benefit of the village, for a period of one hundred years.' *Hélas*, I thought, it's now too late to make the church an alternative offer.

'But out of interest,' the mayor continued, 'had the garden been available, what would you have done in it, grown vegetables?' Yes, I said, I would have restored the *curé's* garden as a *potager*. He smiled. 'Ah, with your lovely English herbs.' An idea struck me. 'Yes, Monsieur le Maire, with lots of beautiful, scented herbs.' Then, choosing my words carefully, I said, 'So why don't I rescue the garden and still grow herbs – that everyone can appreciate?'

His eyes lit up. '*Quelle idée superbe,*' he cried, 'a village herb garden. How wonderful that would be for Saint Montan.' He paused, 'But how much would you charge?' Why nothing at all, I assured him, I'd do it for pleasure. He looked at Suzanne, and she confirmed I was serious. His smile broadened even further and he looked down at the diary on his desk. 'Madame Holt, can you come to the village council meeting next week and explain what you'd like to do?' he asked. I glanced at Suzanne and she was beaming. I agreed to attend the meeting; we shook hands with the mayor and left.

As soon as we were back in the street, she turned to me and said, 'Congratulations! The mayor loves the idea.' But wait, I pointed out, the councillors have to decide at the meeting. Suzanne just smiled and, taking my arm, we walked back to the house. And that's how this story began.

CHAPTER ONE

The First September

STANDING ON TIPTOE, I could just see over the wall. The intense, dry heat of the late summer brushed past my face but the view was blocked by a riot of entwining weeds, their tall stems waving gently in the breeze. To my left, I could make out two raised terraces, while to my right a low, stone wall stretched into the distance following the path of the river below.

My gaze was diverted by a slim, mud-brown lizard emerging from a crevice. It paused, absorbing the heat from the old stones. Then, sensing my presence, it slipped quickly over the wall.

I bent down for my digging fork and, lifting it above my head, threw it over the wall. The spade and rake followed. I found a foothold and hoisted my way to the top, jumping down on to the cushiony weeds. I was about to rediscover the forgotten garden.

The long narrow space had once been a fine *potager* where the *curé* – the village priest – grew his vegetables and fruit. But two decades or more ago, the garden had been abandoned and nature had taken over. Fig trees thrust their way between the stones of a dry-stone wall, and across the narrow gateway an old pear tree, long ago the casualty of a winter gale, was slowly rotting into the ground. A large *micocoulier* tree threw a patch of welcome shade over part of the garden, and nearby I spotted a spindly sapling, probably seeded from a fallen apple but now struggling through the jungle of weeds. The old *curé's* garden had become a haven for wildlife; bees were busy collecting pollen, and butterflies fluttered skywards as the breeze brought down the earliest yellowing leaves from a Lombardy poplar.

IDYLLIC THOUGH the scene appeared, I had taken care to wear my stoutest gardening shoes and moved forward slowly through the undergrowth, watching for any sudden movement of an adder or an outsize scorpion.

But such cares were soon forgotten in the excitement of discovery. I came across the traces of the last gardener's toil, the raised ridges of once-cultivated earth baked hard by the sun of twenty summers. I nearly fell into several deep holes that followed the line of the lower terrace – were they for collecting rainwater? I found the small gardening bothy, or tool store, roofed with the curved terracotta tiles of the Midi, but hidden beneath a riot of wild clematis. Now and again, I stepped on an unseen plant of wild calamint and its clean, fresh scent was released into the warm air as I crushed the leaves. Even in this scene of total neglect, I felt exhilarated by the adventure of making a new garden from the old.

I was making my way around the garden in order to draw a plan of it. I needed fairly accurate measurements of its length and breadth, and the changes in level. For my idea of how to rescue the garden was to be presented to the *mairie* – the village council – at an open meeting in a few days' time. I hoped to be able to persuade them that the forsaken *potager* should now become a village herb garden; I had in mind a tranquil, perfumed space where villagers could linger on a sunny afternoon, and where visitors to the medieval village could stroll and relax in an aromatic sanctuary.

Wielding my metre rule, I managed to flatten enough nettles and hack down rampant brambles to make a reasonable estimate of the dimensions of the garden. As so often in the past, the site had been chosen with considerable care, protected from the prevailing winds by the high rocky foothills of the gorge, yet collecting the water from mountain springs above it. A group of twelve pine trees stood guard like apostles on the steep slope above the garden. Had these been planted by the *curé* to afford some further shelter from the wind? Now mature, these evergreen sentinels provided welcome shade from the fierce meridional sun.

The garden occupies two hillside terraces that run beside, and above, the tumbling stream below. Ardèche hill terraces are

rarely wide, and this was no exception; together they measured only five metres at the widest point, their length roughly thirty metres, though narrowing at the northern end, furthest from the village. Its size meant the garden was properly domestic, which was far more appealing to me than a vast public space. One could relate to this ancient strip of earth and the prospect of turning it into a beautiful place was invigorating. Even though the amount of work involved looked daunting, I felt that the reward would justify it. In the past probably no more than one gardener had maintained the plot, and I began to think that this could be repeated; that the new garden could be created and made by just one individual, despite the fact that the ground would need to be cleared and dug, beds and paths constructed, then filled with the most aromatic plants of the region. That one person was to be me. My plan was to offer to do it.

ARMED WITH CRUMPLED SHEETS of paper and scrawled measurements, I retreated to my kitchen table as ideas for the redesign of the garden began forming. I started with the premise that since Saint Montan is a medieval village, the new scheme of things would need to be in harmony with its past.

This village gives an overwhelming impression of antiquity: the encircling limestone rocks and the medieval buildings constructed from them, the ruined, fortified château silhouetted against the azure sky, the old stone houses clustered at its foot. The earliest-known inhabitant of Saint Montan was a fifth-century hermit who was later sanctified, taking the name Saint

Samonta, and whose cave dwelling, high in the steep rock face of the gorge, still exists.

The oldest building, the eleventh-century chapel named after San Samonta, lies at the extremity of the village at the foot of the gorge, only a stone's throw from the garden. Tucked between them, the Grotte de Lourdes is an open-air place of worship instituted by the village priest at the close of the nineteenth century and, until a generation ago, a shrine where pilgrims came to be blessed and doused by the nearby spring. At one end of the garden the river is fed by the *source de fièvres*, a spring said to cure fevers and still thought to have healing properties; it issues forth unceasing from the rock, even in the driest summer.

People have lived in this village for at least one thousand years, possibly much longer if the Romans (whose road passes between the village and the Rhône) strayed to this site, where springs emerge from the rock and the sky is almost always blue, betraying its warm micro-climate. The valley in which the garden lies is known as *le val chaud* and, as it climbs through the gorge, the trapped heat of summer intensifies.

To harmonise with the existing landscape and the irregular dimensions of the plot, I felt the garden should be fairly naturalistic. Constructing some ornate eighteenth-century conceit such as a *parterre* or a *broderie anglaise* would be both historically inaccurate and out of place. The garden should be simple and appear natural in its setting. Since the site is long and narrow I felt it was more pleasing to divide it into four or five smaller spaces, so that each could assume its own identity within the whole.

Moreover, because the garden is first seen from the road above it and the higher elevations of the village, I began to realize that if each of the smaller gardens were discernible by the colour of its summer blooms, it would look appealing from afar and would also be interesting on the ground. I visualized a bank of lavender with flowering rosemary bushes overlooking the river, scented honeysuckles, climbing roses and wistaria trained against the high dry-stone wall. Reluctantly, I arrested my train of thought and reminded myself that when planning a garden, ideas need to be carefully organized – unless you actually yearn for a kind of cultivated jungle.

I looked around and saw that the man-made environment was characterized by the rectangles and squares of the battlemented wall, and the Romanesque semicircular curves of the doorways and arches. I decided that these two shapes – the rectangle and the circle – should be reflected in the design of the garden. I then set about arranging them in a satisfying way. Equipped only with my straight-edged metre rule and a pencil, I traced circles around the base of a wine glass. I remember rubbing out pencil marks with a piece of white bread until I found an eraser in the village shop!

DESIGNING A GARDEN for public use means a departure from private practice. The paths have to be wider, the perspective of the garden from all points matters even more and the garden must have plenty of interest even for the visitor who cares little for horticulture. But, as with all gardens, the experience of being in it should be one of intense pleasure. The place should delight the senses.

Few gardens offer as many possibilities for pleasure than a garden of scents and fragrance. Although I have spent most of my gardening life growing culinary herbs, I was now able to

expand into the much larger province of plants of all kinds that enchant us with their perfume. And not just from their blooms – but from their leaves, their stems, their seed heads, even their decaying foliage. Few projects have ever absorbed me so totally.

Gradually the scheme I had for the garden began to take shape. Taping together several sheets of ordinary A4 typing paper, I could produce a sufficiently detailed design with an acceptable scale. And I decided that the colours that would characterize each of the four smaller gardens should be cream and white, pink and rosy red, mauve-blue and violet and – at the western end – the sunset shades of yellow and orange.

Now I had to submit my ideas to the mayor and the councillors. For an Englishwoman to advise a French village on what to do with one of their public spaces took a certain degree of – what? – cheek, chutzpah, confidence … I was afraid it might even be seen as arrogance. Fortunately, I was known in the village as an author, and the French editions of my cookery and gardening books were well thumbed in the village library. Soon after I'd delivered my plans and design to the *mairie*, my husband and I entered the council meeting to be greeted with friendly smiles and handshakes. The mayor, Monsieur Carraro, and his deputy, Madame Gaillard, smiled encouragingly.

Saint Montan has always been a most welcoming community. But I felt nervous sitting there as the mayor worked through the agenda, addressing this chamber crowded with villagers. Suddenly I heard my name and nudged my husband to stop reading his thriller, carefully concealed behind council papers.

The mayor invited me to stand and tell everyone about my ideas. Taking a deep breath, I began to describe how I thought the *curé's* old garden could be transformed. Then I sat down and everyone clapped. The French are invariably tolerant, however badly their eloquent language is mangled. The mayor held up the design I'd submitted, though one would have needed binoculars to see it clearly from that distance. He looked at me from across the room. 'Madame Holt,' he declared, 'the councillors held a meeting yesterday and voted in favour of your proposal.' I said how pleased I was, and he announced that at the end of the meeting there would be a glass of Champagne for everyone, to toast the success of the *jardin aromatique* ... and now that all had been agreed, I could start tomorrow!

So I DID. Halfway through the morning, I clambered over the wall and began to rake away the dead grass in the nearest corner on the river side of the garden. As soon as a small area was cleared, I decided to try the ground with the fork. It went in surprisingly easily. I could prise up the first big clump of tangled grass with its matted roots. Oh, the delight of seeing the earth below – it was beautiful, a fine light brown tilth, quite sandy and free draining, but the very foundation of a perfect garden. This was ground that had been worked over again and again for centuries, and I quietly thanked all those gardeners who had gone before me for making my task so agreeable.

Small wonder, though, that the weeds had taken over; the cultivated plot had been well prepared for them. My job now was to recover it. I piled the uprooted sods to one side, and broke up the small lumps of earth with the tines of the fork.

I actually enjoy digging. I like the physical exertion – the lifting and stretching necessary to turn over clods of earth with a pronged metal instrument. I love the look of freshly turned ground, the still-slightly-damp chunks from which one separates the bigger weeds, and then teases out the smaller ones, and roots, as each clump is broken apart. At that moment the tilled earth never looks more appealing – a rich loam perfectly prepared to receive seeds and plants. Aside from this sensual pleasure, I am immensely curious to see what lies beneath the surface of a garden. Sometimes it is simply old roots from trees and shrubs, roots that need to be worked loose and removed, sometimes it is handsome fat worms that improve the ground by digesting it. On occasion I've found hidden treasure – in England I once uncovered a small silver coin from the fourteenth century – but more often on old land one finds shards of broken pottery and china, or fragments of white clay tobacco pipes.

AFTER AN HOUR or so of slow, steady digging, I pushed the fork into the ground and suddenly noticed a large toad near my foot. Every garden should have a toad: he is the gardener's friend who eats small grubs and unwelcome weevils. This one was huge, bigger than I'd ever seen, his pock-marked skin green-fawn, and his hooded eyes gleaming like jet. I stood still and waited for him to jump away. He stayed put, so I bent lower to study him more closely, quietly urging him to jump away. And then I froze. For what seemed an age I could scarcely move. I saw that I had stabbed him, and pinioned him to the ground by one of the tines of my garden fork. I heard myself saying 'I'm so sorry, I'm so sorry', and bent down to extract the metal prong as gently as I could. 'I've killed him,' I thought, 'I've killed this innocent friend.' A small amount of black liquid oozed from the wound but he was still alive. I began to make a shady lair around him with some of the broken weeds and lumps of earth. I hoped if he could stay cool and calm he might recover. I decided to finish digging for the day and slowly returned home.

Next morning, I went back to see if the toad was still there, or, dreadful thought, had died. But he was gone. He might have crept away to die, but I preferred to believe he was recovering somewhere in the thick grass. In the next few months I discovered another smaller toad who still lives in the garden. But it is the memory of that first toad that stays with me, and I hope that he now lives quietly, down beside the stream, well away from the gardener's fork.

Chapter Two

October

OCTOBER HAS ALWAYS been my favourite month. Summer has bid farewell, the nights have grown cooler, and the morning dew gleams like satin on leaves and flowers. The perceptible bite in the air is as appetizing as a glass of chilled Chablis. And when the weather is placid, the days are perfect for gardening – sunny, quiet, balmy even. Yet as the sun's heat fades – relative to its lower angle in the sky – natures obliges: leaves fall and reduce the degree of shadow, making each space seem larger and brighter.

I was making solid progress in the garden, though it may not have looked that way to the passer-by. Large sheets of black plastic covered part of the overgrown ground. During early autumn there is still sufficient heat in the soil for the normal process of decay to work quite quickly in your favour. Beneath the plastic coverlet, the top growth rots down and energetic worms pull the compost into the loam to enrich the humus. Black plastic sheet is often used in southern France, but normally to retain the moisture of newly-planted land.

As the small patch of tilled earth began to enlarge, I would stand further up the garden and look back to where I had worked. Holding one hand against my face to hide the unsightly plastic from my view, I would spend a few minutes visualizing how the garden would look after further cultivation. Probably most gardeners on virgin ground do the same thing. The slow business of digging can make one a touch impatient at times.

It is doubtless contrary to all the rules of professional gardening but, pleading enthusiasm, I decided to move ahead to the next stage of the plan. As soon as I had prepared enough ground to be able to mark out the first beds, I did so. With my metre rule and two pointed sticks cut from a fig tree and joined by a length of garden twine, I set about marking out the White Garden. The design is basically a circle with a border curving around it; not difficult to execute, though it was important to establish the correct position for the central path since this would prescribe the axis of the remainder of the design. Fortunately, I was not constructing a building – nothing was likely to fall down if my measurements were not mathematically exact. That said, even in an informal garden the proportions have to be right. The eye does not deceive, and incorrect alignment can be troubling every time you look at it.

Like a child on a sandy beach, I bent down and began to mark lines on the lightly trampled earth. With one sharpened stick firmly wedged in the centre, and the string measured to the correct radius, I pulled it taut and gently pressed the other stick into the smooth surface. Walking slowly backwards, I dragged the stick around the circumference of the circle. I stood back and surveyed my work. That looked pretty good, I thought. I consulted my plan.

But no, the central path would veer to one side if I left the circle as marked, so I scuffed over the earth and tried again. Not for the first time in the history of gardening, the paper plan failed to work quite as expected when transferred to the field. It was some consolation to think that Repton and Brown must have faced similar problems. Gradually I reached a pleasing compromise between imagination and reality. Elated that I had succeeded in marking out the first section of the garden, and keen to see what it looked like from above, I jumped up on to the second terrace. It was a joy to behold that, just as I'd hoped, the design actually worked. Truly, the garden was beginning to take shape. I began to fork over the earth in the border ready to be planted.

The first plant I moved into the garden had been given to me the evening before when I called on Madame Marquet in Larnas. From the foot of her fine double white lilac she pulled up three promising looking seedlings. I planted the first in the White Garden, against the low, stone wall above the river. Then I scrambled down the river bank and dug up a pretty feverfew with lime-green lacy leaves and white daisy flowers. If this garden were to be a reflection of the village, I wanted to use as

many local plants as possible. I'd seen a sturdy young elder-flower further down in the still overgrown part, so that was uprooted and moved into position. Then, carrying a trowel and a small basket, I began to climb the hillside seeking suitable additions.

THIS DRY, WARM OCTOBER WEATHER had lasted for ten days; we were enjoying an Indian summer, known in France as *l'été de Saint Martin*. Even the grape pickers, the *vendangeurs*, were wearing sun hats. The leaves were turning colour, from bright yellow to ochre, and already the scarlet bracts of the lentisc shrubs flared like flames against the weathered grey rocks.

Tracts of thin earth on the limestone terrain of the Midi support the scrubby flora known as the *garrigue*. Lavender and thyme grow wild on these steep, craggy slopes. Juniper bushes dot the hillside, their spiky glaucous foliage producing hard green berries that take two years to ripen to navy blue – yet the wait is worthwhile since the flavour of juniper berries is irreplaceable in game dishes and for flavouring rich terrines. The plants of the *garrigue* are more aromatic than their cultivated brethren. They develop small, intensely scented leaves, as they struggle against the elements, pushing and threading their wiry roots into crevices between the rocks.

I slowly made my way up the steep hillside, tacking from side to side to lessen the slope, scrabbling from rock to rock. There were no paths, just trails of scree that looked like inviting tracks covered in stone chippings. But once you step on such a treacherous slope, your life is in your feet because the surface is not stable and the sharp, gravelly chippings begin to slide as soon as they are disturbed ... and you slide with them. Villagers tell of childhood escapades when they returned home to a scolding, with their clothes torn and their skin grazed because they descended the mountain by the shortest route – via a scree.

Nevertheless, provided the slope is gentle and you make your way carefully across a scree, you can use these barren areas as a kind of pathway up the mountain. Now and again, in the shade of a rock, you find a patch of bright green, spongy moss, moist from a mountain spring. The moss is easy to cross, provided you can hold on to one of the dwarf blackthorn bushes. That day they were covered in midnight-blue sloes, and I made a mental note to return in a day or so to collect the bitter fruit for flavouring bottles of gin, vodka and *eau-de-vie* in time for Christmas.

Unless you are a mountaineer, it is pretty difficult to climb the steep Saint Montan hills vertically. By choosing easier gradients, I had taken a southerly direction, towards the village, and had arrived on my own land. As I climbed, I gazed down on the largely uncultivated herb garden, and could see all too clearly how much work lay ahead of me.

TEN MINUTES LATER I reached the summit, where a large limestone pavement offered a smooth, dry resting place from which to enjoy the view. The panorama was breathtaking, spreading from the village immediately below, across the vineyards and fields of sunflowers, to the long, broad valley of the Rhône. I could see the A7, the *Autoroute du Soleil*, following the path of the river, hardly straying from one of the oldest routes in Europe; the one that leads from the Mediterranean to the north of France, and one taken by invaders for thousands of years. The ancient Greeks, the Visigoths, the Saracens and the Romans had all passed this way. Somewhere below me was the place chosen by Hannibal to cross the raging currents of the Rhône with his herd of elephants, on his way to the Alps.

I was standing in what was *Gallia Narbonensis*, the huge region of southern France that two millennia ago was occupied and administered by the Romans. Looking eastward to the far side of the Rhône, I could see Roman *Provincia*, the area now known as Provence. From this vantage point, one can see that Saint Montan is, indeed, *à la porte de Provence*. Beyond the Rhône, a long white gash in the countryside revealed the newly-constructed second TGV line that now links Paris and Marseille in three hours – in about the same time, Roman centurions would have marched hardly thirty kilometres. Further on still, the lilac-grey horizon showed the granite crags of the southern Vercors and the pre-Alps as they sweep south to the low cone of Mont Ventoux – the best-known peak of the Rhône Valley.

Hidden from view by a bluff in the hills was the nearest town, Viviers-sur-Rhône, the historic seat of the bishopric that had given the old name to this region of the Ardèche, the Vivarais. The Italianate town, with its magnificent cathedral perched above the river, lies a few kilometres north of the famous *défilé*, the narrow limestone gorge through which the tempestuous Rhône used to burst and bubble on its way to the sea. These days, the Rhône has been tamed by the hydroelectric dam in this section of the river. Yet the *défilé* lies on the latitude that defines the Mediterranean climate, and so significant is this fact that it is shown on a tablet fixed to a wall in Viviers. South from that point – where Saint Montan lies – the climate becomes Provençal; and there the olive will flourish alongside the vine and the fig. I stood up and, carrying my empty basket, began my descent.

RETURNING TO MY QUEST for a sample of each native herb of the region, I scrambled down the steep hillside that forms the wild part of the garden behind our house. I was looking for those plants known in Provence as *les bonnes herbes,* or *bonis erbo,* and valued for their ability to assuage the ills of man, or simply to enhance his pleasure. Fortunately for the gardener, most of these plants are perennial and would form the permanent aspects of my garden. Any annual herbs could be seeded in small spaces, but it is the perennial planting that gives a garden its distinctive character.

I loosened a plant of wild thyme, the pale silver-green *serpolet* of Provence. To my mind, this is the loveliest of all thymes; the soft, subtle shade of its needle-fine leaves and the overwhelming strength of their fragrance cannot fail to endear it to all who know it.

In full sun, and tucked between the weathered boulders, were clumps of winter savory, known here as *poivre d'âne*, donkey pepper. This herb is rarely seen for sale, yet is one of the characteristic plants of the Midi and is used in genuine Provençal cooking. Winter savory is perennial and grows about ten centimetres (four inches) high with slim, pointed leaves; in midsummer, and sometimes again in the autumn, the herb produces small, delicate bluish-white flowers. Lulu Peyraud of Bandol near Marseille – whose robust, lively cooking has been carefully documented by the American foodwriter Richard Olney – uses winter savory almost exclusively to season her dishes. My neighbour, Juliette Rogues, praises the herb for its ability to replace garlic and pepper in a recipe. In fact, the herb is so popular with good cooks that visitors from Paris have been seen to collect huge bundles of it to dry in their urban kitchens for use all winter long in *daubes,* and other slow-cooked meat dishes.

Reaching the lower slopes of the hillside, I picked some sprigs of the wild rosemary, *rosmarinus officinalis*, which grows easily from a woody sprig pushed into potting compost. Close to our house, I uprooted a small clump of the delicately-scented, wild dianthus, *D. deltoides L.* The colour of its fragile pink flowers resembles the cheeks of a blushing young girl, accounting for its charming old name – the Maiden Pink.

Ever since the public meeting in September, neighbours and friends had begun to bring me plants for the garden. Our front terrace now housed quite an impressive collection.

Sometimes the plants would appear mysteriously and anonymously, crammed into a plastic bag and left by our garden gate. Or, hearing a light tap on the front door, I'd step outside to discover a terracotta pot of well-rooted cuttings standing on the top step, and then notice Suzanne Doize's car disappearing

up the road to Larnas. From its very beginnings, Suzanne had been enthusiastic about the proposed herb garden, and had gone to enormous trouble to sow seeds and take cuttings of suitable plants.

In lovely old terracotta pots, she had rooted dozens of cuttings of lavender, rosemary and nepeta in preparation for the borders. Suzanne had also produced four healthy rooted cuttings from an old rose that she says is always planted in cemeteries in the Midi. It has glossy dark green foliage and charming, small, scented blooms, pink-budded, but opening to white. I must try to identify it in my rose books.

Suzanne's sister, Jeannette, had delivered a big clump of tansy with its bright yellow button blooms, and a glowingly healthy French tarragon – that essential herb of *la cuisine bonne femme*.

Monsieur Fauque, who lives in the main street of the old village, and has a small riverside garden, brought a handful of suckers of purple lilac and a hefty root of a particularly aromatic spearmint. As you brush your hands over the leaves, the scent evokes a vision of steaming new potatoes and green peas piled high with melted butter trickling over them. A sprinkling of finely chopped mint, *et voilà* – the perfect dish.

On other occasions, villagers would first pay a visit to the garden then, standing on the road overlooking the site, would take in the unhurried progress, nod their approval, and say, '*Petit à petit l'oiseau fait son nid.*' (Little by little, the bird builds its nest.) 'When are you going to be ready for the passion flower I'm growing for you?' they would ask. 'Quite soon, I hope, perhaps next month,' was my reply. 'Ah yes, *la fête de Ste Catherine*,' they would answer, before continuing their afternoon walk.

Gradually my idea for a beautiful garden planted entirely with aromatic plants and medicinal and culinary herbs was taking shape. I noted on my paper plan where each plant would be placed to advantage and, in time, they were given their permanent home in the freshly tilled earth. It began to dawn on me that this garden was not to be assembled simply from plants purchased in the usual way, from the local nursery or garden centre. These were plants that the villagers thought suitable for the community garden, these plants had been carefully chosen by their donors, because they were considered worthy of this public space, where the delight they give could be shared with everyone.

CHAPTER THREE

November

BASKETS OF RIPE, purple figs and twenty flagons of home-pressed olive oil were given by the villagers of Saint Montan to their priest each year, back in the sixteenth century. Quite when this custom died out is not clear from the episcopal records. But it would be difficult to revive today, since there are remarkably few fig trees in the village, and the olive is even rarer.

Yet, given the historic role of the fig and the olive in the village, it seemed to me apt to include these two fine trees in the planting plan for the *curé's* old *potager*. Moreover, since the church remains the owner of the land, and has leased it to the village for a period of one hundred years, a fig tree and an olive would be particularly appropriate.

A fig tree still flourished in the *curé's* old garden. Perhaps he had planted it, or it could have been self-sown. The tree grows on the upper terrace, about halfway along, and though still quite young, is an attractive specimen. Its big, floppy leaves throw a patch of welcome shade over the lower terrace all summer long.

This left me with the planting of the olive. Such a pleasurable task! No tree is more beautiful, to my mind. Ten years ago I planted six olive trees in my own Saint Montan garden and they

now produce a good crop of delicious ripe, black olives in time for Christmas. In the past, olives were so widely grown in the village that an old rhyme advises picking the fruit on 15 November, the feast day of Saint Montan himself:

Pour Saint-Montan
L'olive en main.

The olive, *Olea europaea*, the most venerable of Mediterranean plants, was probably introduced to Provence by the Phocean Greeks in the seventh century BC. The tree is renowned for longevity – it can survive for a thousand years – and even when cut down will often shoot afresh from the gnarled bole. Though identified with the Midi, the olive is surprisingly tolerant of harsher growing conditions – I have grown a small olive tree in a tub in England for twenty years. But its life is much shorter in a very wet, or very cold, climate.

The evergreen olive tree with its grey-green sabre leaves rustling in the slightest breeze produces tiny creamy flowers in early summer. Its fruit is the substance of legend; its oil, as both food and medicine, is the finest in the world; and a tisane of dried olive leaves is now thought to be a possible treatment for high blood pressure. What's more, a branch of the olive tree is the universal symbol of peace. And though, in time, an olive tree can become quite large, skilful pruning will keep the tree to a reasonable size. On grounds of age and importance alone, perhaps every herb garden in the Midi should have one.

I COULD SEE THAT in the Saint Montan garden there was probably sufficient space for as many as half a dozen small trees of various kinds. They would give height to some of the herb borders and bring necessary shade to the sunniest areas of the garden. After the fig and the olive, the almond is the most representative tree of the region. From its original home in the Far East, the almond is again thought to have been introduced to southern France by the Romans. They used the dried kernels in many dishes, both sweet and savoury, and are even credited with devising the famous sweetmeat of nearby Montélimar – almond-rich nougat.

And, of course, the pretty shell-pink blossom of the almond tree made it a natural choice for the Pink Garden. The flowers appear early in the year – from January onwards, in a mild winter. Part of the crop of green velvet-covered fruit, described as nuts, is harvested in July for eating fresh, when the kernels are still white and milky. The remaining almonds are left on the tree to dry until September, when the shells have become brown and hard. In this state, the nuts can be stored for winter use.

I planted the almond tree close to the low wall on the river side of the garden so that it could be seen clearly from the road. At its foot, I grouped the herbs and aromatic plants that looked well together. I placed a mossy-leaved purple sage next to an upright, cotton-candy pink-flowered hyssop, and tucked behind them a clump of butterfly-attracting sedum, *S. spectabile*, 'Ruby Glow' with its flat-headed blooms. This contrast of form and leaf shape, with subtly varying shades of colour, represents the kind of harmony in planting that is deeply satisfying. Not only were the plants handsome and valuable in themselves, but they would have an effect greater than the sum of their parts. This kind of natural planting, which appears in many English gardens, is rarer in France. I was eager to show that a garden composed entirely of herbs but grown in this way could be just as beautiful as any other kind, and might, perhaps, be more attractive than a regimented design.

A week or so later I planted up the other border in the Pink Garden. A lacy-leaved tamarisk stands at one end with a small congregation around it: two blush-pink hardy geraniums, a clump of coral-pink day lilies and a handful of scented dianthus and cottage pinks in front. Later I shall add one of the wild mauve-pink mallows. In the spring, the gaps will be filled with pastel shades of stocks, thrift and rosy-pink cosmos.

FROM EARLY IN THE MONTH, Suzanne Doize had been reminding me that she would deliver some more plants from her garden on the correct day, the feast day of St Catherine. This particular saint's day falls on 25 November and it is regarded as auspicious by all gardeners in France since it marks the point when the rate of growth is almost negligible. So it has long been considered the perfect time for planting trees and shrubs.

On the day Suzanne arrived with two saplings from her big fig tree – we enjoy its juicy fruits every summer. With them she carried a small tree for the herb garden that is generally known in the Midi as an acacia, though correctly it is a false acacia or robinia, *R. pseudoacacia*. This delightful member of the leguminosae family is used in the perfume industry and grows wild in many parts of the south of France. It is often to be found near streams and water courses as the tree prefers moist ground. And it has the great merit of being none too fussy about ground fertility, since, like other members of the pea and bean family, its roots produce nitrogen.

I have always loved the acacia. One grew in a neighbour's garden when I was a child, and there are few more aromatic trees to be found. The pale green leaves appear in spring, and then the perfumed creamy-white blossom arrives. How often I've stood beneath an acacia in flower just to inhale its heavenly scent! In France, these delectable blooms are dipped in flour and fried in butter to make a lovely summer pudding. A few weeks later, after the flowers fall, decorating the ground as if for a summer wedding, you discover that this gorgeous tree has even more treasures to offer. From midsummer until the first frost, the leaves themselves produce a wonderful fragrance. Walk near a grove of acacias on a dark summer night and they will reveal their presence with their spicy bouquet. And even in early autumn, when the leaves shrivel and turn pale tobacco-brown before falling to the ground, acacia leaves perfume the air. I prefer the wild variety to the hybrid forms since I find it more aromatic, and wonderfully fecund too – once you have one acacia, others will soon seed themselves around it.

ALL OVER FRANCE, the day of St Catherine is marked by tree-planting ceremonies; the television news shows school children, old-age pensioners and amateur gardeners planting small saplings and spindly shrubs amid a smiling throng. It is a welcome and practical reminder of the natural world.

A couple of hours from here, the small town of Saint Jean du Gard – where Robert Louis Stevenson completed his travels in the Cévennes and said goodbye to Modéstine, his donkey – holds a plant festival to celebrate St Catherine. Each year a different horticultural theme is selected, for example, the chestnut, or perhaps the grape.

When I visited the festival recently, the focus was on wild fruits. The town holds not only a tempting plant market, and an exhibition of well-known and rare species, but also a conference, a film show, a painting exhibition and dances. Even the town's restaurants participate by devising special menus featuring that year's theme. I sampled a *salade du pays*: crisp leaves of *endive frisée* and lettuce with a scattering of hot, buttery duck livers and wafer-thin slices of smoked duck breast, dressed with the superb local olive oil and garnished with pillar-box red wild barberries – their sharp sweetness a perfect foil to the duck.

DURING MY FIRST EXPLORATION of the herb garden, I had been struck by the beauty of the wall behind the narrow upper terrace. This hundred-foot-long, traditional dry-stone buttress is built into the hillside, to prevent stones and boulders from falling into the garden, and to give protection from the damaging winds that hurtle over the mountains and down the gorge. As soon as I began to plan the garden I realized this magnificent weathered wall would make a fine backdrop for honeysuckles and entwining summer jasmine, for perennial sweet peas and scented climbing roses. On warm, still days the plants would perfume the air around them in an enchanting way.

Highly fragrant plants have been grown in domestic gardens since records began. The rose and the lily have long had religious significance and were cultivated in monastery gardens as a sign of devotion and purity; indeed, sweet scent itself was once seen as a godly virtue. In fourteenth-century Europe, the secular idea of romantic love emerged with the arrival of the troubadour, a courtly musician from the grand houses of Italy. *Le Roman de Rose,* an epic poem, translated by Chaucer, was illustrated with portraits of gardens showing enclosed areas decorated with rose-covered wooden trellises.

Old-fashioned roses of the past have now returned to favour with gardeners in Europe, North America and the southern hemisphere. In France, they are described as *roses anciennes* and *roses anglaises*, and have become highly fashionable. A few years ago, in the nearby town of Grignan, around the château where Madame de Sévigné penned most of her famous letters, many examples of both kinds of rose were planted and now clothe the towering walls. It is a fine sight in May and June.

Early varieties of roses have many virtues that few of the modern hybrids possess: the blooms are usually of delicate hue, their form is often looser and many petalled, and, above all, the roses are fragrant. In England in particular, rose growers have revived some of the distinguished varieties of the past, and breeders such as David Austin have pioneered the development of new roses that embody these charming old-fashioned qualities. I spent many happy autumn evenings planning which varieties of scented roses would be suitable company for the herbs.

My list included the shell-pink Bourbon rose, 'Souvenir de la Malmaison', with its offspring, the faded apricot, 'Gloire de Dijon'; I would plant it alongside the creamy-white 'Alberic Barbier', and the rampant but engaging 'Albertine'. Naturally, there should be examples of the fragrant centifolias, both the white and the red 'Rose of Provence', and the gorgeous baby-pink 'Fantin-Latour'. I've always had a soft spot for climbing single roses such as golden Mermaid and pale peach 'Meg',

and – if I couldn't find it in France I would bring one from England – the delightful, white-flowered 'Rambling Rector', an appropriately named rose for the former garden of the *curé*.

I LEFT MY ORDER FOR ROSES with Monsieur Braize, the local nurseryman, who would phone me when they were ready. To make room for them, I broke off from digging the main terrace and began to tackle the narrow upper one.

These long, narrow terraces are typical of the distinctive, stepped terrain of the Ardèche and the Cévennes. Centuries ago, small tracts of level ground were hewn from the steep hillsides of river valleys. Even today, majestic chestnut trees and trailing grape vines are still cultivated in such precarious places. The valuable pockets of earth are held in place by traditional stone walls skilfully constructed without mortar.

Though just as overgrown as its larger brother, the upper terrace was somewhat easier to tackle. Since the wall casts a shadow during the afternoon, the ground does not dry out as readily as elsewhere on the plot and thus is easier to dig. Moreover, the terrace hugs the hillside and is better protected from the Mistral.

In its days as a *potager*, this terrace had been used for growing *les primeurs* – those early season crops such as finger carrots and golf-ball sized turnips that are harvested when young, tender and so delectable. The earth had been tilled and fed regularly for generations and, though neglected for a long time, still produced a beautifully fine tilth as soon as the top growth was removed. Quite quickly I was able to clear and prepare a narrow strip of cultivated earth almost the whole length of the wall so that I could begin to establish the climbing plants at its foot.

By the end of the month I was ready to plant the bed of thymes. Many years ago I had visited Hexham Herbs in Northumberland, home to the British National Collection of Thymes, and I had not forgotten how fetching is the thyme clan. My friend Jeannette drove me to a good plant nursery in La Drôme, the nearby *département* across the Rhône, and we chose a dozen highly aromatic examples. I arranged them, still in their small plastic pots, on the prepared ground. Each plant was no larger than the palm of my hand and I hoped to be able to make a kind of thyme carpet which could be walked over by children and the partially sighted, who I thought might appreciate the fragrance of the herbs released into the air as they are crushed underfoot.

Planting herbs specially to be trodden on was popular in England during the reign of Elizabeth I, particularly in paved courtyard gardens. The crevices between the stone slabs were planted with creeping and low-growing herbs such as the carpetting thymes, pennyroyal and camomile. It is quite easy to keep the herbs fairly flat by trimming them when needed with secateurs or kitchen scissors. In my experience, these herbs flourish as a result of such manicuring, growing dense and compact, almost like cushions of fine lace.

Chapter Four

December

I WOULD NEVER HAVE BELIEVED how cold it can be in the south of France. But this was December, and gardening required a padded jacket, corduroy trousers, thick gloves and a fleecy balaclava. Only my eyes were exposed to the chilling air – I looked like a terrorist! But I was determined to complete the digging before the end of the year. Luckily, after working for ten minutes or so, I felt surprisingly warm and could withstand the cold for a couple of hours.

Though there was not much more terrain to clear, it was, unfortunately, the most overgrown. Even the last gardener had rarely penetrated this furthest corner. The brambles, or wild blackberries known as *ronces*, had thrown up long, whippy branches studded with huge hooked thorns that caught on your clothing and, if not careful, your skin, making painful puncture wounds. Robust seedlings of the native *micocoulier* tree had thrust deep roots into the earth. And the ground was peppered with big cushions of couch grass that had to be prised from the earth before one could dig below them.

The *mairie* had offered to spray the weeds and turn the earth with a mechanical digger. Though momentarily tempted by such a solution, I declined. I garden organically and I loathe the practice of adding lethal chemicals to the earth. Furthermore, I knew from bitter experience how these machines can not only break up the ground, but also chop weeds into myriad pieces that often regrow. There is no substitute for digging by hand and foot.

THE VIRTUES OF traditional digging have always been appreciated. St Fiacre, the patron saint of gardening, received as his garden (possibly with a little celestial help) as much land as he could surround with a spade-dug trench in one day – because spade-dug ground, as opposed to ploughed earth, has long defined a garden. A thirteenth-century English tithe document described gardens as 'curtilages dug with the foot on which dwellings stand'. The speed of digging by foot was reckoned by William Cobbett, the eighteenth-century campaigner for home-grown food, to be such that would cover two-thirds of an acre in eight days. Needless to say, Cobbett would have despaired of me. I was far slower.

Every half an hour or so I would pause to catch my breath, and in the age-old gardening custom, I leaned on my fork and looked around. With my back to the prevailing wind, my gaze took in the sombre silhouette of the ruined château with a couple of tapering cypresses tilting in the wind. I noticed how my own tallest tree, a sweet bay, now reached beyond the height of the house eaves and must measure ten metres (about thirty feet). Its roots have found water from the stream, and it is now as high as the tallest bay tree I've ever seen in England – the massive specimen standing left of the doorway of Fowey parish church in Cornwall.

Legend surrounds the serenely handsome bay: it is said that a bay tree protects a house from evil spirits and therefore should be planted near the door. The herb's botanical name, *Laurus nobilis*, indicates its origins as a regal plant, the leaves fit even for a crown. Laureates received the wreath of dark green satin leaves as a mark of honour. Julius Caesar, it is said, attracted criticism for parading his bay wreath rather too often – though friends claimed he did so simply to hide his baldness.

Quite why there are so few bay trees in English gardens is hard to fathom. Aside from their use in the kitchen, the leaves give off an attractive balsamic fragrance of lemon and nutmeg almost all year round, and it is particularly pronounced on warm dry days when the essential oil is released by the merest breath of air.

The bay is remarkably hardy, though cold, dry winds can scorch its leaves; but when planted in a protected site the tree grows lustily and tolerates poor soil. Its home is the Mediterranean region, where both fresh and dried bay leaves are used freely in the

kitchen. In classic French cooking, one bay leaf tied with a sprig of thyme and a few leaves of parsley is the ubiquitous *bouquet garni* used to flavour soups, sauces and many slow-cooked dishes.

ALL YEAR ROUND, but principally in December, I make bay wreaths as presents for friends. Starting with a 60–80 centimetre (23–30 inch) length of heavy-gauge green garden wire, I bend it round to form a circle, twisting the ends together firmly. I cut sprigs of bay leaves and prune the tree at the same time, by cutting off bigger branches from which to strip the end shoots needed for the wreath. Then, using lengths of thin florists' wire, I attach the sprigs to the wire frame. A bay wreath usually looks more attractive when the leaves all run in the same direction.

When the frame is completely covered with leaves, it is a good idea to make a wire hanging loop at the top, and either leave the wreath plain, or add a raffia or ribbon bow. The wreath can be used for decoration over the festive period, and then moved to the kitchen, where the aromatic leaves are detached as needed. As the bay leaves slowly dry and their colour fades, their flavour intensifies.

WHEN YOU GROW your own herbs, you don't just use them for cooking, or as cut flowers for scenting a room. I like to send greeting cards made with fresh or partially dried herbs. For this

I buy plain, pale-coloured cards and cut them into squares or rectangles. Then I punch two holes towards one side, or in one corner, through which I thread a ribbon to secure the herbs, before finishing with a knot or a bow.

A sprig of rosemary is appropriate for sending to loved ones since it symbolizes remembrance and fidelity in love. Bay leaves, on the other hand, which were the emblem of immortality in ancient Rome, make a suitable decoration for a birthday card. Or, I might choose some stems of flowering lavender, to indicate faithfulness – the language of plants was once so well known that in Shakespeare's Romeo and Juliet, when the Nurse says, 'Does not rosemary and Romeo begin both with a letter?' (i.e. the same letter) the audience appreciated the significance.

As I worked my way to the far end of the upper terrace in the herb garden, clearing the undergrowth before digging the ground, I uncovered several piles of oyster shells, some wine bottles and the site of old bonfires.

In one place a few charred pages of a book lay stuck together, still protected by the overhanging wall. I took off my gloves to examine them: they were pages from a missal giving suitable prayers for each saint's day, and were printed in Latin.

Suddenly I was transported back to the days, decades earlier, when the garden had been the village priest's *potager*, and Latin was the language of the Tridentine mass. This was evidently where the garden boy disposed of the rubbish from the *presbytère*. I pondered that a life revolving around a Latin missal, French wine and an abundance of oysters was far from unattractive. The church clock woke me from my reverie, repeating each hour as it struck, as church clocks so often do in French villages.

On the morrow I raked together all the dry bramble branches to burn them on the old bonfire site. The air was still, and the grey-white plume of smoke rose in a straight column; when it reached the height of the surrounding hillside, a light breeze made it drift away from the garden and towards the village.

The undisturbed upward path of the smoke showed just how protected this garden was from the prevailing air currents. I looked back at the part that was now cultivated and planted. I could see some lavender and hyssop still in bloom, the sage, *Salvia neurepia,* alight with scarlet flowers, and even a recently planted buddleia, *Buddleia fallowiana,* had braved the winter air and put forth some orange-centred creamy blossom. Close by, the honeyed scent of the Japanese medlar, or loquat, was a midwinter treat. The olives on the small tree had fully ripened and were now sooty black and ready to pick. I paused, taking a few slow, deep breaths at such a pleasurable sight.

Even though I enjoy their primitive appeal, I try to have few bonfires. In a heathy, organic garden, I prefer to compost all surplus vegetative matter. However, the recent acquisition of a most useful machine has slightly changed my tactics. In the village herb garden, apart from the trees and the roses, the plants need little feeding, for most herbs thrive on poor soil. Moreover, I wanted the plants to live a normal, unpampered existence – the way plants always have. The garden was intended to be a natural part of its environment. So rather than fertilizers, the ground requires a mulch to retain moisture during the high heat of summer and to counteract the dessicating effect of the occasional, but year round, Mistral wind. This is where a leaf machine is invaluable.

An electric leaf grinder not only tidies up the garden by vacuuming up the fallen debris, but after crushing the dry leaves, it yields an attractive mixture that resembles oversized tea leaves. This makes a perfect mulch for spreading around plants and over bare earth, with the double advantage of retaining moisture and suppressing weeds. It is a convenient home-produced mixture that could even be used for making paths if you had enough fallen leaves to hand. This garden, though, would need paths laid with stronger stuff to withstand the measured tread of herb-lovers.

I BEGAN TO THINK about the garden paths. They had to be wider than in a private garden, and so they would be that much more noticeable. This made the choice of material an important consideration since, in total, it would occupy a fairly large area. Although brick paving is sympathetic in a small herb garden, it is not really suitable for a limestone region. Smooth pebbles or cobbles set in mortar also work well in small gardens, but can be difficult to walk on in a large one, and wooden paths, although pleasant underfoot, naturally look best in a woodland setting. Finally, I decided that small chippings or gravel would be the most appropriate choice for the paths since it would echo the surrounding bare rock and stony screes.

I have put down gravel paths in several gardens. The material is admirably hard wearing, it drains well, it looks natural, and when it begins to look scruffy, gravel can be spruced up simply by raking. The main disadvantage is its tolerance of weeds.

For organic gardeners – only a generation or so ago there was no other kind – chemical treatments are unacceptable, so one way of combatting weeds on gravel paths is to put down first a layer of landscape fabric, a loosely woven rot-proof material that allows water to pass through, yet discourages seedlings from emerging. The few tiresome weeds that do appear can be raked or hoed away. Or, in dry weather, I have used that remarkably simple but ancient method advocated by Albertus Magnus in the thirteenth century: boiling water. Of course today I just carry an electric kettle of hot water into the garden and pour. But while I do so, I like to imagine how weeds were killed this way centuries ago – by using the stone-age method of dropping stones heated in bonfires into wooden buckets of water, again and again, until the liquid boils.

BY THE MIDDLE OF THE MONTH I had succeeded in digging all of the ground on the two long terraces. This had uncovered a small pool at the far end of the lower terrace which collected spring water through a narrow channel carved into the rock. Beyond the pool lay the one small area of garden still to be cleared and cultivated – a raised island of tall weeds where our cats had made a summer camp, in places flattening the dry grass into cushioned nests. Even today in the biting cold, Palmer, our

most adventurous cat and my constant companion, came outside to check what I was doing in 'his garden'.

It was a kind of reward – and a great relief – to discover that clearing this elevated, though much neglected, area of the garden was easier than anywhere else. Perhaps weeds had been thrown up here by earlier gardeners, because the earth was rich with humus, and in two days I had cleared and dug over the ground. It is, in fact, the perfect place to sit and paint the garden, protected from the wind and looking towards the village. But it is not easily accessible, so I decided to turn this aspect to advantage and make it an island of exotics. I earmarked it for some unusual plants and herbs, that ought to be kept out of reach due to their prickly spines or inedible berries.

I had my first plant for the exotic island ready and waiting to be transplanted. I'd acquired it a few months earlier when our friends Marie-Frédérique and Rémi Tiberghien arrived for lunch carrying a huge cactus. The prickly pear, *Opunta vulgaris*, couldn't have looked lovelier. The plant had twenty large buttercup-yellow blooms, and many more buds waiting to open. 'It is too dangerous where it's growing in our garden,' they said, 'close to where our grandchildren play.' The plant's painful-looking spines could indeed inflict a serious injury. 'So since it is a medicinal plant we thought you'd like it for the *jardin botanique*.'

After planting their cactus I remembered that our neighbour, Alphonse, had offered an agave, a native succulent of the Americas. This huge, spiky specimen had seeded unexpectedly years ago in his hillside garden and now he had two small agaves ready to plant. I struggled up the slope, cautiously dug it from its home on a rocky outcrop, and transplanted it near the cactus.

Then René Soufflard, a Saint Montan friend interested in the culture of India, arrived with what he described as a 'cardamom plant'. It resembled a small-leaved palm, and René thought it was fairly tender. So it would go well on the exotic island in the summer, and then overwinter in a sunny corner of my side terrace. It could nestle alongside the big clump of lemon grass, *Cymbopogon citratus*, which I had been nursing for five years since we spent a sabbatical term in Malaysia. Tender tropical subjects like these are best placed in a garden for the summer only, well embedded in the earth but still in their terracotta pots.

When I next visited our nurseryman, I brought back for the exotic island a yucca, a fine mimosa, 'Quatre Saisons', and a magnolia *soulangeana*. Then Jeannette Doize dropped by. She was growing some odd-looking mandrake seedlings and would bring me a couple when they were larger. The mandrake, *Atropa mandragora*, once known as Satan's Apple, would be a fine choice for the island. The plant has garnered so much legend and fable, that for us to know exactly where the truth lies is – fortunately, perhaps – fairly difficult to establish. Quite quickly, the herb garden's island of exotica was beginning to look interesting.

Chapter Five

January

For a few days at the turn of the year, the herb garden receives no direct sun. The orb lies so low in the sky that its rays cannot reach the ground at the foot of the gorge. And so the garden sleeps in the long shadow cast by the steep hillside.

There is, though, plenty of reflected light. The winter sunshine ricochets off the weathered stone of the medieval walls and the ochre rock of the restored houses around the château. I'm struck by its purity, its dazzling brilliance that illuminates so clearly every protruding corner and cleft in the stone, while back in the garden it accentuates every bud and tentative leaf. Because, of course, growth has not ceased, it is simply slower: the curiously contorted flowers of witchhazel, *Hamamaelis mollis*, emerge from their bare, tawny branches to fill the air with an intoxicating scent, and the blushing pink blossom of *Viburnum fragrans* opens ahead of its pleated, bronzy leaves.

Then towards midday on the sixth of the month, glorious sunlight cascades over the brow of the hill and grazes the top of the low wall beside the stream. From now until December the sun – unless obscured by cloud – will be in the garden everyday. I feel like a Druid celebrating the return of this benificent god, proclaiming the end of the shortening day and the too-long nights. In response to this glad incandescence, the mimosa tree I've planted in the furthest corner of the garden breaks into a triumphant sunburst of scented yellow, and for the first time in my life I pick armfuls of fresh mimosa to take into the house instead of those mean little sprays sold so expensively in England.

A SMALL SPACE LIKE A HERB GARDEN cannot depend on massive swathes of planting and impressive architectural effects such as pleached beeches and *allées* of nut trees. The Saint Montan herb garden is of domestic size and that, to my mind, is the essence of its appeal.

I hoped it would illustrate some of the many graceful and attractive ways of creating a garden in a relatively small space. To hold one's interest, the planting should not only be carefully considered but also contain some pleasing, yet less familiar, horticultural examples that could inspire other gardeners.

The French tradition for topiary, for instance, was one that I wanted to reflect. Woody herbs that can make appealing topiary subjects are myrtle, lavender and small-leaved box. Box, *Buxus sempervirens,* is one of the principal plants of the *garrigue*. Used medicinally in the past, we now know that the leaves are highly toxic, their active ingredient working in a similar way to quinine. In my own hillside garden there were several large box bushes, and around them plenty of self-seeded plants. I transplanted four and decided that instead of just letting them grow untamed, as in the wild, I would trim them into a more controlled shape.

Clipped trees and bushes have been prized by gardeners since classical times. Fifteenth-century French engravings show examples of topiary. Popular shapes included the tree pruned into graduated tiers – known in Victorian times as a cake stand. Others were trimmed into a pyramid, or sphere.

Once you've decided the style of topiary for your chosen shrub, you can, of course, clip and prune it simply by eye. But if you prefer more accurate geometry, then a wooden or wire frame tied to the central spine of the young plant is helpful. Topiary frames can be bought at garden centres, or you can make your own. The idea is to construct a shape with a few horizontal spurs that define the dimensions of the final topiary. You prune the fresh shoots to the limits of the frame, eventually allowing the dense growth to cover it completely until hidden from view.

One of the attractions of topiaried herbs is that the trees can be of miniature form – not as dwarf as a bonsai, but certainly a

manageable size; a small one could even be trimmed from a wheelchair. I'd grown a straight-stemmed rosemary from a cutting, and thought it would make a good subject on which to practise my topiary skills.

Potted up and placed on a work table, the rosemary plant was about to undergo a transformation. Inspired by an illustration from a book on medieval gardens, I hoped to produce an '*estrade*', a three-tiered rosemary bush that tapered towards the top. I took a metre rule and placed sticky tape at intervals to mark the distances for the horizontal 'plates' on this intended 'cakestand'. With my smallest secateurs I began to clip the shoots. Leafy branches were to be left in three places with the remaining stem of the plant trimmed bare to make the 'trunk' of the tree. Cutting the foliage immediately released the herb's beautiful perfume. Herb topiary, I discovered, is yet another aspect of herb garden pleasure, and I now understand how some people become so fascinated by the craft that they tend their cherished plants every day.

A FEW WEEKS EARLIER I had potted up a couple of young bay trees that had seeded themselves from my large, mature tree. The seedlings were 50 centimetres (20 inches) high, yet their stems were still pliable. On one I trimmed away all side shoots, leaving the bushy topknot: in time the tree would become a standard bay with a well-trimmed ball of leaves at its head. The other bay tree I planned to shape into an obelisk. This involved pruning the side shoots, allowing the lower ones to be longer and therefore wider, gradually trimming the rest more severely towards the top. The taper could be flat-sided or curved like a cone – either is comely – but looking at the natural growth of the tree I decided a cone would work well and began to prune it into a straight-sided circular taper.

Another trick that I wanted to try was to weave together three plants, plaiting or twisting their pliable stems to make one central 'trunk'. For a dramatic effect you can do this with two or three different colours of the same variety, such as an hibiscus or two green-leaved sweet bays with one yellow. Or, you could entwine a summer jasmine around a standard lemon verbena.

As ever, French gardeners are imaginative in this respect, even going so far as to bend the stem of a young bay tree around a chestnut pole so that the trunk becomes a spiral. The pole is removed once the plant's trunk has become rigid. But I shall need to wait until another of my bay tree seedlings grows tall enough to try this.

Nevertheless, in some parts of the garden I planned to have faster growing examples of trained plants. In these cases, trailing ivy would be used to clothe a wire frame. For a small garden, or even a terrace, carefully trained and trimmed ivy can be most appealing.

So I set off with a trowel into the wooded valley upstream from the garden to dig up rooted strands of ordinary ground ivy, *Hedera helix*, though for anyone in a city this idea works equally well with small pots of decorative trailing ivy bought from a garden shop. When buying ivy, it is worth looking out for interesting varieties such as 'Parsley Crested', whose green

leaves redden in the winter, and 'Anne Marie', with grey-green foliage splashed with cream.

Choose a medium-sized terracotta or stone pot that has one or more drainage holes. Take a length of stout, green garden wire and measure from each end the depth of the pot and a little more; leave these 'legs' straight at this stage. Then carefully bend the rest of the wire into the shape that you want. Even a simple circle works well, but I rather favour a spiral. You may be able to bend the wire into your chosen shape straight away or a solid former such as a log might be needed for bending it around. A spiral that tapers towards the top gives an impression of movement and also makes the topiary more stable.

When you are happy with the wire shape, place it in the pot with the two ends protruding through the drainage hole, then bend them away from each other against the base. Now place a layer of gravel in the pot and fill with a peat-free cuttings compost, or a mixture of loam and sand, making sure that the topiary shape is positioned centrally. Finally, transplant at least two ivy plants, placing each fairly near the wire frame. If the trailing growths are long enough, start to train them up the wire, if necessary securing with small, green wire ties.

Within a few weeks the ivy should have begun to clothe the wire frame; trim off any errant sprigs or train them into the main shape. Depending on the size of the frame and the growing season, the ivy-clad topiary shape should be covered within the year. The pot can stand directly on a gravel or paved surface, or it can be placed in a border – provided the rim of the pot lies just below the surface.

A MORE AMBITIOUS VERSION of the same idea of an ivy-clad topiary is to make an archway. This works particularly well over a gateway or at an informal entrance to a garden. The frame can be made from cut saplings bound together with garden twine or green string, or from heavy-gauge wire secured firmly to the ground, or fence, or low wall. The basic frame can be wrapped in chicken wire if you wish to achieve a bulkier form. In Barcelona one Christmas Eve, I admired a complete nativity scene created this way in topiary, with the figures and animals rooted into the ground and the ivy leaves trimmed short to cover the wire frame. Evergreen, ivy-clad gateways are quite popular in France and there are one or two handsome examples in the old part of Vaison-la-Romaine – but remember that to look their best all topiary shapes should be kept well tonsured.

THE FINAL DAYS OF JANUARY bring a foretaste of spring. Deliciously mild weather with bright sun and no wind means that I can garden without a coat. Glancing up at the ruined château I notice that on the ramparts, Christophe Mathon and Les Amis de Saint Montan are restoring the wall, bare-armed in teeshirts and jeans. (L'Association des Amis de Saint Montan was founded thirty years ago and is a group of volunteers and benefactors dedicated to the restoration of the medieval village and its château.) When weeding, I discover the first ladybird of the year, and while sunning himself on the dry-stone wall, our small ginger cat suddenly shrieks with delight as a tiny lizard ventures from its winter home and then scuttles away.

Though grateful for this particular vagary of the weather, I know it would be foolhardy to begin sowing and planting outside – February could yet be bitterly cold. The lengthening days encourage me, instead, to sow seeds for germinating on the kitchen windowsill. This annual thrill is a timeless, primitive instinct that all true gardeners share – a deep desire to replenish nature's bounty.

Living in the south of France has made me a devoted fan of the marjoram and oregano family. In his *Oxford Companion to Food*, Alan Davidson points out that 'it is questionable whether the term oregano (or origano, as it is sometimes spelled) should be treated as a plant name. Tucker (1994) argues persuasively that oregano is best considered as the name of a flavour'. Like many cooks, I find that oregano is a uniquely valuable seasoning for pizzas, flat breads and many salads. But it is worth looking out for seed of some of the choicer varieties of marjoram that can now be sown in pots early in the year and placed in a glasshouse, cold frame or warm windowsill.

Into some 10 centimetre (6 inch) pots of seed compost I sowed a few grains of knotted marjoram, *Origanum vulgare*, 'White Anniversary'; a newish variety of this perennial herb that I wholeheartedly recommend. This cultivar is an excellent addition to the herb garden, strongly aromatic and healthy. It withstands quite parched growing conditions and even flourishes in terracotta pots on a sunny terrace, or in wooden tubs as a foil to summer geraniums. This handsome herb stays good-looking all year round, producing tiny white flowers in early summer followed by curiously rectangular, segmented seed heads which usually last all winter. I simply tidy up the plants in the spring by giving them a light back-and-sides haircut, and at the same time look out for self-sown seedlings which can be easily potted up for transplanting, or giving to others.

Another attractive member of this herbal family is golden marjoram, *O. vulgare*, 'Aureum', with its bright yellow leaves.

Although less strongly aromatic than its green-leaved sister, it still has immense charm and a pleasing habit of making puffy hump-shaped cushions in the herb garden. But for flavour the finest of all marjorams is Dittany of Crete, *Oreganum dictamnus*, with its lovely, woolly leaves and tiny, tubular, pink flowers.

In other pots I sowed seed of purple-flowering chives, clary sage, summer savory and the true lavender – which, in a good year, will flower in late summer. And, like most years, I also sowed pots of old-fashioned scented sweet peas and nicotiana.

BREAKING THE RULES – this should have been done last summer – I take some cuttings of the perennial, large-flowered nepeta, *N. cataria, var. faassenii,* for planting out in late spring. Commonly known as catmint due to the state of near ecstasy it produces in most felines when they brush against it, the herb has little use in the kitchen other than to deter insects, though the wild form is sometimes used to make a tisane. The herb's medicinal virtues, however, include a treatment for insomnia, as is the case with camomile.

Catmint is a prime subject for the perfumed garden, where it looks cool and elegant planted as a carpet beneath white scented roses, or when used to edge a long, paved walk. In his celebrated garden at Gravetye Manor in Sussex, William Robinson, the nineteenth-century author, planted a narrow border of nepeta opposite one of purple-flowered lavender. Gravetye's present owner, Peter Herbert, has faithfully maintained this magnicently perfumed walk.

Chapter Six

February

'Everyone in the rhône valley likes the Mistral,' said my neighbour, Juliette Rogues, as I stood shivering on the front porch. 'We much prefer it to the rain. The wind blows away the damp and dries everything up – just look at that lovely blue sky.'

True enough, no cloud could withstand the freezing gale that was blowing from the north, so the sun shone brilliantly. The infamous wind – its name means 'master' in the Provençal language – is often accorded a capital M. It blows mainly in the winter. Dry, cold air sweeps down the Rhône Valley from the Massif Central when the pressure is high over the mountains but lower in the valley. The Mistral occasionally blows in the summer, too, and although something of a nuisance as it rattles the shutters and whips up dust, it is naturally not as bone-chilling as in the winter. 'The Mistral always blows for three, six or nine days. *A bientôt*,' added Juliette cheerily as she set off for the village shop. I start counting the days. I shall never be really Ardèchoise – I'll never learn to love the Mistral.

Even in the vineyards, where work has to be done almost every day of the year, only half a dozen people were bent low over the vines. You have to be pretty hardy to work in the full thrust of the Mistral. Luckily, I found a well-protected corner of the herb garden, hard against the hillside, and was able to continue pruning roses and shrubs. It was a slight consolation to hear the gale blowing far harder on the hilltop as it tore across the barren plateau straight from the snow-covered Cévennes.

UNTIL NOW I HAD MARKED OUT the edge of each bed simply by digging down vertically with the spade, to make a shallow trough between the smoothly flattened path and the border of tilled and raked earth. But I knew that in the long term some better solution would be called for. If the paths were to be grassed, the clean-cut edges could have stayed, and the contrast between mown lawn and growing plants would have been sufficiently bold and satisfying. But because the paths were to be gravelled in the spring, a more deliberate edging to the borders was required.

I first experimented with small, flat sheets of smooth stone, evenly cleaved and eroded from the hillside, then carried down into the river bed by winter storms. But although the material was impeccably local – *du coin*, in fact – and therefore a natural choice, the effect was too jagged to look satisfactory. I also found that it was difficult to keep such small pieces of stone permanently upright – either the wheelbarrow, or my feet, would push them flat – so maintenance might be a problem.

The familiar edging of dwarf box hedges I had already rejected as too tedious to maintain, and anyway not appropriate for a medieval village. Early manuscript illustrations of French herb gardens often show the borders edged with narrow planks of wood. The method is perfectly sound provided the borders have straight sides, but in the Saint Montan garden I had designed many borders with curved edges. Then I remembered a fifteenth-century French engraving depicting a low, woven trellis or wattle placed around the borders of a small *herbier*. Once this had dawned on me as a possibility, I became attracted to the idea. I decided to practice.

WILLOW AND HAZEL TREES are reckoned to produce the best slim, young growths – osiers or withies – for weaving into baskets. Neither of these trees grows near the garden so I looked around and noticed the crop of long, thin suckers, or water shoots, thrown up by the big old fig tree over the wall in my own garden – these would be fine for experimentation. I cut the shoots from the base of the tree and carried a bundle into the herb garden.

Years ago, I had woven myself a willow shopping basket and I remembered that the long, slim withies had to stand in water to keep them sufficiently pliable. But these freshly pruned withies were still supple – so much so that milky fig sap began to run from the cut ends.

Using secateurs I cut some short lengths, about 15 centimetres (6 inches) long, from the stoutest of the sticks. I spaced them about 12 centimetres (5 inches) apart along one side of a border, pressing them vertically into the earth, leaving about half the length above ground to form the uprights. Then I took a long withy and placed it on the ground, allowing it to protrude past the 'end post' at the corner of the border; with one hand holding the withy in place, I began to weave the rest

in and out of the uprights. I was amazed that the withy stayed put, half expecting it to jump out of position.

I took another and repeated the process, but this time weaving the withy on the opposite side of each upright. With five withies in position, the trellis was just high enough to provide an edging that was distinctive but not obtrusive. I trimmed the uprights level with the top withy, then stood back and admired my handiwork. 'It's going to work!' I shouted, somewhat surprised! I walked a little further away to get a better view of the woven edge. It looked exactly right for the garden – in perfect scale, in the appropriate material and naturally weathered. Soon I had used all my own withies, so I cut some from Alphonse's mulberry tree, and then set off for the village with my secateurs, each time bringing back bundles of thin wands.

So far I'd only made the diminutive trellis in a straight line. Now it was time to tackle a curved edge. I found that placing the uprights a little further apart helped to accommodate the weaving; it allowed the withies more room to bend in tune with the edge of the border. Again, I found the result sympathetic:

the trellis gave such a natural look to the border, its colour was a muted green-brown, and its form set off the plants behind it like a well-judged frame around a painting.

A woven trellis makes an attractive edging to borders in a herb garden but it does use a great deal of material. Every time we drove out of the village I took my secateurs so I could cull any withies I spotted. A good place to find them is usually near rivers where the trees grow fast, and the best kind, as basket-makers know, are willows, with their flexible young shoots.

The following week the garden gods once again bestowed their blessing: the workmen from the *mairie* decided to prune the weeping willows in the middle of the village, just as I needed more osiers. I had a word with the chainsaw expert and he set aside all the pliable branches. My husband offered to collect them, which meant a morning spent tying the whippy stems in huge bundles in order to drag them along the village street to the herb garden.

So inspired did i feel by the new woven edges, that a week or so later I decided to become more ambitious. I've always wanted to grow a green trellis, a medieval bower of cool willow leaves with a shady seat below. To do this one needs willow saplings. If you have a garden with moisture-retentive ground, just slips of willow pushed into the ground will grow. In Saint Montan, where the terrain is mainly dry, gardeners do it differently.

'Impatience and gardening do not go well together,' wrote Vita Sackville-West. But if nature gives you a helping hand, it might not be so, I thought, as I walked beside the river in the centre of the village, where most of the Saint Montan willow trees grow.

The willow is such a thirsty plant that if you cut a stem and place it in fresh running water it develops roots astonishingly quickly. In the village I had often seen slim willow wands – about a metre (yard) long and as thick as a broom handle – left on the riverbank, or propped up in one of the roadside fountains that are fed by springs, with their cut ends standing in the cool running water. In three to four weeks, the base of each stem develops a mass of fine white roots. Hey presto! An instant tree! Even Vita might have approved.

I cut a dozen slim branches of weeping willow and left them loosely tethered to the riverbank beside the herb garden, their feet dipping in the water. Each day I looked carefully for signs of growth. In two weeks, fine white hairs had emerged, and after another three weeks the roots were strong enough to withstand transplanting. Then I marked out the ground exactly where I wanted the arbour, bearing in mind that I would place a wooden garden seat under it later in the year. I planted the rooted willows in the shape of an open rectangle, with four willow saplings on each side, and four between them across the back. To prevent wind rock, I gave the saplings extra support with some chestnut palings.

As they grew, I tied in willow cross struts to make a grid. When they were tall enough I bent the tops of the saplings towards each other and tied them together to make a curved roof. In time, the living trellis becomes sufficiently strong and the supports can be removed.

The growing trellis idea can be adapted to make a summer 'green house' – planted in a circle or a rectangle, with a door and a roof – fun for children to play in. Alternatively, a willow house makes a sightly home for a compost heap or piles of spare pea sticks. Other quick-growing shrubs such as cotoneaster and eucalyptus can be also used in this way, but the willow grows fastest.

Provided your ground is well nourished, climbing plants can be encouraged to ramble over a live green trellis. A grape vine such as *vitis* 'Brandt' is attractive, or the yellow hop, *Humulus lupulus,* 'Aureus', looks lovely trailing over a willow arbour. If you prefer a climbing rose, then the blessedly thornless, fondant pink and fragrant 'Kathleen Harrop' is ideal, possibly planted alongside a favourite clematis: *Rose, rose and clematis, Trail and twine and clasp and kiss,* wrote Tennyson.

SHADE IS ESSENTIAL in the summer in the Midi: hence the thousands of plane trees that cast their cool, gauzy, green light in squares and streets across the south of France.

In a herb garden one of the prettiest ways of creating shade is to plant two wistarias, one on either side of a garden seat. If you choose one blue/mauve-flowered variety and make the other white-flowered, you will have created a gorgeously perfumed summer retreat. To begin with, the wistarias will need vertical support, but in time the twisted trunks of these magnificent plants will support themselves and can be trained to meet in the space above the seat.

ONE SUNNY MORNING towards the end of the month, I walked into the herb garden to find what looked like hundreds of small, orange pen tops scattered over the ground. Completely mystified, I picked one up and saw that it was a thin plant membrane that had curled itself into a slim cone. A few more 'pen tops' suddenly drifted down from the sky, and looking up, I saw that the huge Lombardy poplar was shedding the sheaths as its buds burst. I'd never lived so close to a poplar tree before and was unaware of this spring-time phenomenon.

By now the intensity of the sun was encouraging leaves to unfurl on many of the plants. This is the excitement that gets me outside early every morning – there is always fresh overnight plant growth to be admired.

In the White Garden, which had been planted in October, several plants were already looking well established. The small strawberry tree, *Arbutus unedo,* was displaying its delicate bells of white flowers. The lemon verbena, neatly pruned last month, was putting out dozens of fresh, pale leaves. The French use this herb in a refreshing tisane, which is not only a pleasant digestive, but also a highly recommended treatment for symp-toms of the common cold. Small bunches of fresh lemon verbena are often sold in outdoor markets, and packets of the

dried leaves, labelled *verveine*, are usually available in grocers and supermarkets. I like to flavour ice creams and custards with this lemon-scented herb by first infusing two or three fresh leaves in the warm cream, before straining and cooling the mixture. The herb's delicate, scented flowers are pretty enough to decorate a summer pudding, or for adding to a posy of herbs on a bedside table.

Already the white bush roses had plenty of healthy young leaves and the scented white climbing rose, 'Pax', was in bud. Two grey-leaved artemisias, southernwood and wormwood, were producing sprightly shoots from their well-trimmed stems. The wormwood, the variety used for making absinthe, the powerful alcoholic drink now banned in France, was doing specially well; perhaps because Saint Montan is only a few kilometres from Aiguèze, the birthplace of the inventor of absinthe, where a commemorative plaque in the centre of the village reads:

**DANS CETTE MAISON A VECU DE 1706 A 1776
HONORE AGREFOUL, DISTILLEUR-INVENTEUR
DE L'ABSINTHE PLUS CONNUE DE NOS JOURS
SOUS LE NOM DE 'PASTIS'.**

Grey-leaved plants relish the hot dry climate of the Mediterranean, and many have a felted or hairy foliage to limit transpiration during the heat of the day. I can't have too many grey-leaved plants in a garden; they contribute a restful and calm atmosphere. And mixing them with white flowering plants can give a magical, almost moonlit effect.

In the White Garden I have planted a young eucalyptus that I shall keep well trimmed so that it produces plenty of its pretty round leaves, rather than the bigger oval kind that appear on mature growth. Another grey-leaved plant with a distinct and appealing form is the perennial chrysanthemum *haradjanii*, known in France as the 'Marguerite d'automne'. This is a valuable ground cover plant with such deeply-cut leaves they resemble a silver-grey fringe. It enjoys a dry, parched border, and I've grown it on top of a low stone wall where it will eventually become a soft floppy cushion.

Close by, I've placed one of my favourite evergreen scented shrubs, *Pittosporum tobira* with its dark-green, glossy leaves and heads of creamy-white tubular flowers. It is in a sheltered corner, protected by the low-roofed bothy and my own garden wall. Though widely used for hedging in gardens in the Côte d'Azur and elsewhere along the Mediterranean coast, it also makes a fine specimen plant for a mild climate.

I first encountered this pittosporum in Fréjus twenty years ago, when I picked up a cutting a gardener had left from pruning a long hedge. Carried home to England in my sponge bag, I was surprised that the well-travelled sprig took root and grew into a magnificent bush. Planted in a wooden tub in a glazed porch, it filled the space with its seductive magnolia-like fragrance each spring. I can think of few more perfect shrubs, and if you come across a *Pittosporum tobira*, I would urge you to carry it off.

In the centre of the White Garden is one of my baby bay trees, its slender trunk bare of leaves as I train it into a mop-head standard. Around it I've constructed a square of small box plants. These I shall prune into a square shape, so that I end up with a box box – of course, the pun only works in English, though I daresay the French will appreciate the horticultural result.

CHAPTER SEVEN

March

THE FAMOUS BOOK OF HOURS, *Les Très Riches Heures,*
illuminated early in the fifteenth century for Jean, Duc de Berry,
provides some of the earliest firm evidence of French gardening. The country year it depicted, month by month, reveals
absorbing horticultural details like vine-covered arbours, fenced
borders and well-pruned trees.

The portrait for March shows a gardener scattering seed over
the ground and, in the Saint Montan herb garden, the tasks
remain unchanged; they are still carried out by hand and by foot.
But these days of early spring are still too short for all that has to
be done at this time: tilling, sowing and planting await, now that
the sap is rising and growth is active.

Even more satisfying, perhaps, is that many of the plants I'm
putting in are much the same as those grown six centuries ago.
Aromatic herbs are largely unaltered, most having escaped the
attention of the hybridizers – perhaps they realize these plants
are already perfect. The cult of the new, however, and the
fascination for bigness and bright colour in flowers have meant
that some of the old-fashioned fragrant plants – such as richly
perfumed sweet peas – have had their scent sacrificed for size.
But at last the virtues of the older forms are being appreciated

again, and there are now nurseries and seedsmen who pride themselves on preserving these historic and valuable varieties, sometimes labelled 'heritage', to remind us of their past.

The child in us likes sowing seeds and, whatever one's age, the wonder of their germination never fails to excite. My old wooden box of seeds, the harvest of decades, is open before me. I spread its contents over the floor: there are dozens of coloured packets, sealed envelopes, small twists of paper and countless empty film cases that rattle with dried seeds. This is the very stuff of dreams. Half-used seed packets with brief messages scrawled on them date from my Devon garden – they revive countless memories of West Country springs, of horticultural hopes, and not a few happy successes. Even when past their sowing date, if the interior foil pack is resealed after use, some seeds can remain in growing condition. Others can be particularly time-sensitive and lose their zest for life quickly. On the whole, though, it is more often damp rather than time, that destroys them.

There are packets of seeds from Thailand, from Spain and Italy and Greece, from Israel and Turkey, from Cyprus and Malaysia, from all the places I've visited or lived. Most of the seeds come though, naturally enough, from Britain and France.

Tied with raffia is a bundle of short-season herb and vegetable seeds that I remember buying in the old-fashioned premises of the Denver Seed Company in Colorado. I hope the place is still there – it reminded me of Suttons when they had their big shop in the centre of Reading, Berkshire, with its long wall of magnificent wooden seed drawers. A bright picture of the purple cone-flower, *Echinacea purpurea*, now popular in homeopathic medicine, lies on top. I drop it into my basket of seeds to sow in the Pink Garden. From the same Denver seed house there is a packet of evening glory or white moon flower seeds – ideal for those who enjoy the twilit garden. These I'll sow in pots for easy transplanting.

For sowing in situ I choose seeds of clary sage with its pink, mauve and purple bracts that can 'bedizen' a salad – as advised in old cookery books. Into my sowing basket also go packets of fragrant mignonette, blue and red-flowered flax, sweet rocket, night-scented stock, eschscholzia and cornflowers.

Then I consider any gaps in my seed supply. Do I need extra seeds of aromatic plants? Do I have an excuse to go out and buy even more, to indulge in my favourite form of shopping? Sense prevails; I remember that the Saint Montan herb garden occupies only a small fraction of a hectare. So, since the sun is shining, I decide to sow the seeds that are to hand, and to postpone any further purchases until my next shopping expedition.

BACK IN THE AUTUMN when I had started clearing the neglected garden, I had uncovered a series of mysterious holes in the ground; four small basins about the size of a kitchen sink but three times as deep. I suspect this is to allow a watering can to be submerged in them. The basins are built of stone, lined with smooth concrete and joined together by a straight, narrow channel. This gently sloping conduit begins at the far end of the garden as an outlet from the pool which collects rainfall. It runs

the length of the plot, along the edge of the lower terrace and beside the low stone wall of the upper one, and eventually disappears under a stone wall into my own garden. This was the original irrigation system for the former *potager*.

Variations of this pattern of cistern and conduit can be found all over the Mediterranean: in the paved orange tree garden at one side of the cathedral in Seville, for example, and in the tiled courtyards of Fez and Marrakech, while in *The Odyssey*, Homer writes, 'and through the garden plots and orchard ran channels from one clear fountain'. In England, the device was used in some of Edwin Lutyens' garden designs, most memorably at Hestercombe House in Somerset.

In the south of France where rainfall is low, it is only sensible to store water in cisterns for summer use. If need be, the water chamber is constructed underground to reduce evaporation, but if you are fortunate enough to have a cistern fed by a spring then it can be above ground, as in the herb garden. Water cisterns that hold running water usually also have a way of redirecting the water past the cistern when it is full so that the stored water can reach the ambient temperature before being used in irrigation. Though we might enjoy a cool drink on a hot day, plants do not.

Keen to discover the source of the water that irrigates the herb garden, I followed the path of the conduit upstream. It first runs underground in an old terracotta pipe which ends in a grating for holding back fallen leaves, then the channel becomes an open duct, clearly man-made and cleft from the solid rock. The U-shaped channel follows the curve of the hillside until it reaches a sharp turn at the foot of the Grotte de Lourdes. Here, under a mound of bright green moss, a spring trickles from the rock. I bent down and cupped some of the water in my hand – it was icy cold and tasted as water should, of almost nothing.

Beyond the right-angle turn, the channel widens and follows the edge of the stream, running under the footbridge to the Grotte de Lourdes and crossing to the big cavern under the San Samonta chapel. All winter long, water gushes from the cold dark stone – as if Moses had just smitten the rock. Long ago, some devoted gardener had carved the water conduit so that the crops in the old *curé's* garden could flourish. It was humbling to see it; cracked and broken here and there, yet still working and bringing the life source to the raised walled garden.

As I STROLLED BACK into the garden, Monsieur Armand, the president of Les Amis de Saint Montan, arrived with a visitor to the village. We walked among the small beds of plants, stopping to pluck a leaf here, or to inhale the fragrance of a flower there. I talked about the old water course and he remarked that there were several others in the village. It was, it seems, an ancient right of villagers to be able to take water for washing and for plants from the water channels of the village. The conduits were

usually constructed to run along behind a row of cottages, and it was the duty of each householder to keep the watercourse clean and sweet-smelling – it was, of course, forbidden to use it as a repository for rubbish.

Gravity-fed water conduits with supply pipes for separate houses can be seen in the remains of Roman towns in the south of France, Italy and Spain. On one side of a lane leading out of Saint Montan, the vestiges of a medieval tannery have been found where a similar series of man-made stone pools, simply larger versions of those in the herb garden, direct the flow of spring water from each leather-washing basin to run downhill and join the course of the river.

A FEW RAINY DAYS in the middle of the month moistened the ground nicely for planting. There were still gaps to be filled in the borders and along the base of the high stone wall. In a mature garden the plants normally cover the ground so that no bare earth can be seen. In this way the plants create perfect growing conditions, shading the ground and discouraging weeds. Initially, however, plants must be spaced with enough room for future growth. This does have the advantage that, for the first year or so, annuals can be sown in the gaps, which gives more variety to the gardening scheme, and an opportunity to try other plants.

In the Pink Garden much of the basic shape in the planting has been done. The almond tree was in bloom for the first time with its pretty porcelain-like flowers, and the demure and lovely daphne *D. odora* was producing its rich hyacinth-like perfume. I'd transplanted a seedling Judas tree, *Cercis silaquatrum*, which grows wild in the village; it was about to break into its astonishing purple flowers that appear on the bare branches, followed by the lovely greenish-maroon leaves. The tamarisk foliage rippled in the breeze, and the cerise-flowered tree peony was already in bud. The highly scented roses – a deep crimson 'Etoile de Hollande', the 'Apothecary's Rose' (*Rosa gallica officinalis*), whose perfume is the basis of Attar of Roses, and the cream-splashed 'Rose des Peintres' – were in glossy full leaf. Some of the footsoldier plants around them, including the sages, sedum, hemerocallis, cistus and malvas were looking promising.

I HAVE THE IMPRESSION that there are more pink-flowering plants than any other. Perhaps it is simply that commercial growers and florists recognize that pink is a highly popular colour. Consequently, gardeners have plenty of choice in this part of the spectrum.

One of the most stately of pink-flowered plants is the acanthus, with its beautifully sculpted leaves and towering spikes of pink and mauve blooms. Native to the Mediterranean region,

there are several large clumps of the plant growing on the roadside in the village, and one of them had been flattened by a clumsy driver a few days earlier. On my way to the baker's I inspected the damage and decided that some of the broken roots could be nursed back to health in the herb garden. Though the leaves were once used as a treatment for gout, they are famed for the inspiration they gave to classical builders – the capitals of Corinthian columns are often decorated with acanthus. But because a mature plant can grow to a metre (about three feet) in width, I planted my ailing roots at the back of a border where the serrated, slightly spiny leaves would not scratch a passer-by.

Pinks themselves, one of the most engaging of plants, are a natural choice for this area of the garden. Both pinks and carnations are members of the dianthus family, a species long revered in aromatic gardens, from the paved courtyards of ancient India, to the medieval enclosed gardens of Europe. In the past, carnations were often grown in pots for displaying outdoors during the summer, and for overwintering undercover in porches and arcaded walks. Once known in England by the delightful name of gilliflowers, pinks have traditionally been planted under cottage windows so that the lovely clove-like scent can drift into the house.

Dianthus range in colour from cream to heliotrope, but most are, in fact, pink. The flower may be single or double, and the group known as clove pinks have the most pronounced perfume. In flower from midsummer to early autumn, and happy to grow in sandy, alkaline ground in full sun, no garden can have too many dianthus to my mind. Low-growing pinks, with their smooth-stemmed glaucous foliage, can provide a pretty and fragrant edging to a border, reminiscent of those planted alongside a path in a traditional cottage garden.

In the middle of Saint Montan, in a shady corner beside the *lavoir,* the communal wash-house, there still grows a large clump of soapwort, *Saponaria officinalis.* Now that most homes possess a washing machine, the *lavoirs* found in towns and villages across the south of France are rarely used. It is extraordinary, though, how the soapwort plant still lingers alongside them. This perennial herb, with pretty fondant-pink flowers, contains saponin, a chemical that can replace soap and produces a similar lather. Until detergent arrived and soap became cheaper, soapwort was used for washing delicate fabrics such as lawn and organdie. The herb can easily be grown from a cutting, so I snipped off a short length of one of the creeping rhizomes and took it back to the herb garden.

Since pink is such a 'hot' colour for flowers I think it needs to be well spaced with other leafy tints – either grey or green, or, surprisingly perhaps, red – the deeper and complementary colour is not only an effective foil but also softens the pinks. For year-round attractive ground cover alongside pink flowering plants, the red-leaved bergenia, *B. cordifolia,* 'Purpurea' is a good choice.

Oddly enough, though, red-leaved herbs are more often medicinal or culinary than aromatic. I had already planted a crimson-leaved sorrel, mainly as a curiosity since I'd not come across it before. In the spaces between the perennial plants I sowed some red orache, purple-leaved basil and the lovely bronze-maroon perilla with its frilled pointed leaves, described by Joy Larkcom, in her book on oriental vegetables, as the quintessential Japanese herb. It grows easily in the Midi and is often to be seen hugging the base of a stone wall in a narrow shady street. I hoped that once sown it would seed itself in future – *au volontiers,* as my neighbours say.

HEARING SOME VOICES as I worked, I glanced up at the road. Four people were leaning on the low wall overlooking the herb garden. One woman had her arm outstretched and was tracing the curved outline of the borders with her hand, talking animately to her companions. In my English way, I carried on working, as if unseen, and quite soon they continued on their walk. Until there is a proper entrance to the herb garden it is difficult for a visitor to enter. In time, a bridge will be built over the stream, and a sign erected to indicate that this is a public place. Until then, visitors to the village might well assume that the village herb garden is my own private province. And in a way, for the moment, it is.

CHAPTER EIGHT

April

TODAY THE AIR FEELS soft and warm, like swansdown caressing your skin. The current of air is produced by the Sirocco, the wind that blows from the south – from the Sahara and the Maghreb. Is it imagination that seems to bring the scent of spices from the souk, and the sweetness of Mediterranean blooms, on the gentle breeze?

As I walk through the gateway into the herb garden, the part furthest from me is aglow: sunshine yellow is unquestionably the colour of spring. Rich buttercup-yellow Spanish broom, with its gorgeously heavy scent, is in full bloom, with the paler, more delicate coronilla in front. Both grow wild in this limestone country. Curved wands of forsythia and star-faced euryops bloom, with dwarf daffodils and pale primroses at their feet. The enchanting buttery-yellow rose, 'Comtesse du Barry' – named after the famous mistress of Louis XV – which has continued to bloom right through the winter, is still producing flowers. But the scene stealer is the creamy-yellow, button-flowered *Rosa Banksiae* that thrives in the climate of northern Provence.

Here and there are contrasting notes of mauve, pink and white. My magic carpet of thyme is in full bloom. And nearby I cherish a small group of tiny white narcissus – a garden version of the beautiful wild variety that grows in huge drifts on the western slopes of the Cévennnes.

Bees, which have been in the garden on warm sunny days since February, are now working the flowers in earnest. From the time when I kept a couple of hives in our cider apple orchard, I've loved and respected these insects. Since, by tradition, you should tell your hives all the news of the household, I'm still accustomed to whispering a greeting to any bee that comes close. Curiously, it does seem to have a calming effect on these tireless workers, whose devotion to their task, though simply instinctive, is so admirable.

Even with so much in flower, April remains a tidying month, and a horticultural version of spring-cleaning is usually necessary. Last year's dead stems, pockets of fallen leaves and the persistent, over-wintering weeds such as groundsel – I'm told that Leonard Woolf (husband of Virginia) used to maintain that groundsel was evidence that the devil existed – need to be moved to the compost heap.

Once done, you find fresh patches of earth just waiting for plants. So I am able to transplant some of the seedlings of annuals I've been raising in pots: the pale-flowered tobacco plants, white lavatera and Shirley poppies.

Even the nepeta cuttings I took in January have produced strong enough roots for planting out. I set them 25 centimetres (10 inches) apart – they quadruple in size during the summer – around a young specimen ginko tree in the Blue Garden, opposite a gap in the wall that, in due course, will become the public entrance.

In the adjoining borders a few tiny, sky-blue perfumed sweet violets are still in flower. Dark blue hyssop and clary sage are in full leaf. The pinnacles of mauve flowers, with their intriguing musty fragrance, make this sage one of the more spectacular of summer flowering herbs. Soft-blue flag iris are in bud, and will likely bloom by the end of the month.

Against the low wall overlooking the river, I've planted a chaste or hemp tree, whose mauve-blue flowers will appear in late summer. The chaste tree, *Vitex agnus-castus*, is an attractive deciduous specimen for a small garden, with its smooth, grey bark and scented leaves. Less often planted today, it is thought to have been widely grown in monastic herb gardens for its libido-suppressing qualities. A few days after planting the tree I was amused to notice that the blue passion flower (though taking its name from the Christian, and quite other, passion) planted further along the wall last autumn was probably close enough for its entwining tendrils to eventually embrace the tree of chastity – *c'est la vie*.

Now, with the garden looking fairly pristine, I have a first-rate excuse for the choicest form of retail therapy – purchasing plants. Though soon jaded by supermarkets and conventional shops, I am never too tired for a trip to an open market or a plant nursery.

From Saint Montan you can visit a different market each day of the week. Some are just small affairs, held in the village square where local growers and nearby gardeners bring produce to sell.

One of the itinerant cheesemongers or a local *charcuterie* then sets up a stall alongside, and *voilà*! – with a loaf from the village *boulangerie*, and a bottle of wine from the nearest *caves*, you have all you need for a perfect meal.

And lest you fear that, under threat from the supermarkets, this market tradition is dying out in southern France, one village nearby initiated a small weekly market just three years ago. It is now a regular, and popular, feature. Outdoor markets are one of the glories of the Midi; although they continue all year round, it is, of course, during the spring and summer that they benefit most from the climate.

The markets I prefer to go to each week are the ones in the nearest towns. I can choose from Viviers (Tuesday), Bourg-Saint-Andeol (Wednesday) and Pierrelatte (Friday). Especially during the summer, it pays to get there early – not long after 8 o'olock in the morning if you can – when the best produce is still available. The earliest spears of freshly picked asparagus, bundles of crisp-leaved sorrel and sun-ripened tomatoes, the first velvet-skinned apricots and scented white peaches, neat little punnets of perfumed *fraises des bois* and small, fragrant Charantais melons . . . you can't fail to eat well, and cheaply, too.

All three markets have splendid displays of plants for sale. Sometimes I just stand and gaze at such a heart-warming sight.

There are lusty young seedlings of every kind of summer vegetable, from aubergines to globe artichokes, from tomatoes to cardoons, lettuce to leeks. Summer herbs take up half the space on some stalls, and again the choice is impressive – the best flat-leaf or continental parsley, French tarragon, dill, summer savory, sorrel, chives, chervil, lovage and all manner of thymes and sages. Pretty well every culinary herb is here. And, of course, the final destination, the very *raison d'être* of the produce on these admirable stalls is *la bonne table*. I feel so at home here.

Before noon, all this booty has been spirited away by the gardeners of the region. By nightfall, each plant will be languishing in the freshly tilled plots, walled gardens and magnificent *potagers* of the district. My friend Jeannette Doize cultivates one of the finest and most imaginative kitchen gardens for kilometres. She often leaves a box of dew-fresh vegetables on my doorstep, and so tempting are these finger carrots, pencil-slim *haricots verts* and crunchy lettuces that it is hard not to start nibbling straight away. Tucked into a corner is a bunch of the usual French herbs with sprigs of this year's garden experiments, such as Indian temple basil or maybe Vietnamese coriander, or there's a pretty posy of edible flowers, whose petals can be sprinkled over salads. Jeannette is not only a devoted gardener – in high summer she can be seen tending her *potager* soon after dawn – but she is also the most superb cook. How often, in southern France, these two talents ride together!

COMPARED WITH southern Britain, spring arrives here six to eight weeks earlier. And some days in April can even feel like like summer – towards the end of the month I have recorded temperatures nudging 25°C (75°F) in the shade.

So with the season advancing, I have to complete the planting. There remains one prominent area to be worked on. This is a circular bed immediately to the left as one enters, slap in the centre of the Blue Garden. I had always visualized it full of lavender, one of the most aromatic plants of the region. The border is intended to act like a welcoming greeting to the visitor.

The wild lavender that growns on the hillside above the herb garden is the original lavender, praised by Pliny and Dioscorides, taking its name from the ancients – *lavare*, to wash – because of its use in bathing. It is known botanically as *lavandula officinalis, l. angustifolia* or *l. vera* and is characterized by short, stubby growth with slender, silver leaves and delicate heads of flower. The long, slim blooms are usually pale mauve, but they also appear in shades of light blue or pale pink, or even white.

This is *la vraie lavande*. Still gathered by hand from steep rocky sites, it was once the only lavender grown in the Midi. True lavender is hardy and can flourish in the most inhospitable of sites, pushing its roots into tight crevices between rocks, and producing highly fragrant leaves and blooms. Its essential oil has a fine, delicate but lasting fragrance which is preferred by high quality *parfumeurs*.

Until seventy years ago this was the only lavender grown commercially in France. Then *lavandin*, sometimes still known as *lavande bâtarde*, was discovered and identified in a perfume laboratory in Grasse. *Lavandin* is a natural hybrid, produced in the wild by bees and other flying insects. It is a cross between *L. officinalis* and *L. spica* and is readily identifiable by its neat, hummocky habit and bright purple-blue flowers. Commercial growers like it because it can be grown easily in rows, and the flower spikes can be harvested by machine. Although, kilo for kilo, *lavandin* flowers produce a greater quantity of essential oil, it has a less subtle perfume.

The local nurseries mainly offer three varieties of lavender, all of which can be found growing wild in the Midi. *Lavandula dentata,* also known as maritime lavender and once classified as *L. stoechas* because its flower is similar, has distinctive fretted leaves and tufted heads of flowers. While this is an attractive lavender for the garden, or for growing in pots, its essential oil is considered of little value. Spike lavender, *L. spica* or *L. latifolia,* named after its long willowy stems with pairs of flowering spikes and wider flatter leaves, grows well in limestone country but prefers a sheltered site at lower altitudes than the true, more hardy lavender, *L. officinalis.*

And so I ordered from M. Braize no fewer than sixty plants of true lavender for edging the upper terrace, a score of *L. dentata,* a handful of *L. spica* and the same of *lavandin* for the round bed. Since these are the lavenders of the Midi they should thrive. Provided I plant the shorter variety around the margin of the border with the taller varieties in the centre, there should be no need for the knee-high trellis edging that one sees in medieval illustrations. As the season proceeds, lavender does indeed spread luxuriously with the long flower stalks splaying in all

directions. Though this is in itself a charming tendency, it is worth bearing in mind when planting the herb near a path.

During the winter I had experimented with some of the hybrid lavenders that will grow easily in southern England – the pretty fern-leaf lavender, *L. pinnata* and the large-flowered *L.* 'Sawyer', but sadly they failed to survive the rigours of a Saint Montan winter. I shall try these lavenders again, along with my favourite hybrid, 'Hidcote', this time planting them in pots to overwinter under cover, since I'd like the herb garden to contain as many examples as possible of this totally beguiling scented plant.

THE CIRCULAR BED of lavender needs a centrepiece, I decide. I've thought long and hard over what to plant here. The usual choice in the south of France is an olive tree, the grey-green of the foliage toning well with that of the lavender. But this planting duo appears on so many roundabouts and city gardens that I think something different is called for. I like the idea of a yellow or red-leaved shrub, or perhaps a small tree. A corkscrew hazel or a medlar would look attractive, I think, but, as with the olive, I've already planted them elsewhere in the herb garden and I'm loathe to move them now that they are both doing so well.

Then reading Christopher Lloyd one evening reminded me of the virtues of the various elders. In my Devon herb garden, I found that the fern-leaf elder, *Sambucus* 'Laciniata' looks lovely surrounded by herbs. Equally fine is the red-leaved elder, *Sambucus* 'Purpurea'. I shall look for either or both. You can't have too much fragrant elderflower – all that thirst-quenching cordial, wonderful sorbets and muscat-flavoured gooseberry jam.

Chapter Nine

May

The first of May is a holiday in France, and it is the charming custom to mark the first day of summer by presenting to your loved ones posies, and small pots, of sweetly scented lily of the valley, *muguet des bois*.

At eight o'clock in the morning, mist still masked the hills in Saint Montan, removing the familiar horizon. The effect was eerie and dramatic. Walking into the garden, it felt as if the place had been transported to a flat plain. Deprived of its normal setting within the encircling rocky hillside, the garden looked quite different, and I discovered its design afresh, seeing its composition of shapes, its planting patterns and its variation in height with an altered view.

As I stood there, the sun's rays began to filter though the low cloud, quickly dispersing the gauzy veil. Then it was as if the curtain had risen and I could see the colourful stage set – the garden in its full glory in the bold morning light.

In the clear air, the leaves and blooms shone like gemstones. The lime-green, lance-like leaves of lemon verbena wafted their perfume as I brushed past. In a few weeks their lacy flowers in the palest of pale pinks would emerge. The blooms, like those of most culinary herbs, are edible. A delicate cloud of lemon verbena syllabub served in a slender stemmed glass and adorned with a tiny sprig of the fairy flowers is a bewitchingly lovely dish, romantic enough to melt the stoutest heart.

In the White Garden, a Small Tortoiseshell butterfly landed on the flowering philadelphus or mock orange. Then another settled on the bed of flowering thyme, and began to collect pollen. Another arrived, then another. As the air temperature rose, more of these beautiful creatures descended from the hillsides. They appeared like out-of-season snowflakes floating down in the warm, still air onto the aromatic plants. I spotted two diminutive, startlingly bright Blues, then a gaggle of Clouded Yellows on the sedum. In planting the garden I've always had the interests of butterflies in mind. Many of the well-known plants they feed on are in place – buddleia, sedum and yellow alyssum in addition to the flowering herbs such as lavender, thyme and hyssop.

I resolve to plant even more butterfly-attracting plants on the wild hillside beyond the herb garden, and beside the path leading to the garden. It would be wonderful to have a rainbow of delicately hued butterflies floating in an arc above the garden.

I remember how Rachel Carson, the author of that prophetic book, *Silent Spring*, in the last summer of her life and knowing she was dying, loved to watch the magnificent Monarch butterflies resplendent in the Maine countryside. For, of course, these fragile creatures that play such a crucial role in the ecosystem are also a sensitive barometer of its health. May the time never come when butterflies abandon the herb garden.

NEXT DAY the *mairie* workmen arrived. Monsieur Wyss, the stonemason, explained that now was the time to start building the bridge over the stream that would give public access to the herb garden.

They began by digging a rectangular hole on the far bank of the stream, a few feet above the water level. The hole immediately filled with water from the many underground mountain springs in this part of the village. Despite the inundation, by the end of the day they were able to lay the foundation for a strong pile to support one end of the bridge.

After a week or so a wooden arch was lowered into place, one end on the pile, the other resting on an emplacement in the herb garden itself. This was the former upon which the bridge would be constructed. 'This bridge will be built the way the Romans did,' said M. Wyss with a smile of quiet pride, 'entirely of local stone and paved with small cobbles.' The men worked steadily and carefully, never hurrying, and at this time of year the heat of the midday sun is so fierce that a two-hour lunch break is advisable.

Some people sleep soundly through their siesta, others simply close their eyes while resting in an easy chair. I usually begin with good intentions, book in hand, reclining on a swing seat in the shade of our big fig tree, only to discover some time later that remarkably few pages have been turned. The virtues of the Mediterranean diet are now so well-known that they scarcely bear repeating, yet I often wonder whether the proselytisers have not got the wrong end of the stick. It is the daily siesta that makes for a long and healthy life for those who live on the shores of the Mediterranean, for few things reveal such deep respect for a civilized, unhurried way of life as that legendary period of post-prandial rest.

A fortnight later, the bridge could be crossed, albeit gingerly, its surface still rough and uneven and the cobbles yet to be put in place. Each day, interested villagers took their late afternoon stroll via the bridge. They paused and admired its elegant curving line, the skill with which M. Wyss had cut and set the stones. And we had joked about his carving his initials on the hand-hewn key stones at the apex. The future of *le petit pont de Saint Montan*, as he called it, looked secure.

I AWOKE TO THE SOUND of an engine. Was it a tractor passing or a low-flying plane? I looked at the clock and saw it was 2 am, and gradually I realized that the noise was not moving away. I leapt out of bed and threw open the shutters to find that the onslaught was deafening. It was the sound of water, vast quantities of water, cascading in a terrible torrent beneath my window. After a weekend of continuous rain, the river was in spate.

The first thing I thought of was the bridge. The wooden former was still in place and would be an obstacle to the colossal force of the water. I threw on a coat and still in my slippers and nightclothes ran out of the house and down the garden to see what damage had been done. As I ran through the rain-soaked garden, I forgot I'd left the upturned wheelbarrow on the path. After struggling to my feet and abandoning my slippers in the muddy ground, I reached the bridge.

It was hard to believe. I stood there in the pouring rain, staring at the sight. The bridge was holding. The wooden former had moved slightly, but was still in position. The rushing, tumbling water simply took a path around the far end of the bridge to flood the bank, where it was uprooting saplings and dragging tree roots from their mooring. Truly this was a bridge worthy of the Romans. Just as a few years ago the beautiful stone Roman bridge at Vaison-la-Romaine had held against the tragic flooding of the River Ouvèze, now M. Wyss's much smaller bridge in Saint Montan was holding up against the unleashed turbulence of the water.

The next morning M. Wyss arrived to check on how his bridge had fared. He hadn't lost a wink of sleep over it, and was still confident even when he came upon the flooded streets in

the middle of the village. But he began to dismantle the wooden former to allow the river to follow its proper course. By the end of the morning his fine bridge was revealed in all its glory. People came to look at it and admire its grace and strength. Children ran to its highest point to watch the water crashing beneath their feet. Slowly during the next couple of days the river level dropped, and things returned to normal. But the limestone rock of the river bed had been scoured by the flood and shone creamy-white beneath the clear rushing water. And now, *après le déluge*, we also had a splendid new entrance to the herb garden.

I COULD WHEEL MY BARROW over the bridge in order to dump stones and weeds on the far river bank. And visitors could reach the garden itself instead of admiring it from the road. After its soaking the ground was still very damp, and so, acting on the old wisdom of 'sow in dry, plant in wet ground', friends and neighbours began to arrive with even more plants. Suzanne Doize brought seedling Iceland poppies and rooted cuttings of the white perennial candytuft, Juliette Rogues gave me young plants of mauve cosmos and yellow calendulas she had raised in pots on her terrace. For the yellow garden, Susan Beazley, an English friend with a holiday home nearby, arrived with some seedlings of Jerusalem sage, *Phlomis fruticosa*, and a rooted cutting of St John's Wort, *Hypericum perforatum* – a medicinal herb that has recently become a fashionable anti-depressant.

Parts of the garden were beginning to look properly stocked. The thyme bed, for instance, was growing so fast that every morning each cushiony plant had stretched its fern-like fingers further across the bare earth. Soon, the plants would be touching and I would need to place large stones between the thyme plants to keep them separate.

By now, there was little space left in the herb garden for additional plants but, like most avid gardeners, I am always keen to add a few more choice subjects.

On her evening stroll, Juliette Rogues had mentioned a village herb fête she'd read about in *Le Dauphiné* that she thought I might enjoy. The next morning I found she had left a newspaper cutting about it on the front steps, under a stone. We decided to take a day off and go in search of the fair.

THE VILLAGE OF LE PUY SAINT MARTIN lies in the foothills northeast of Montélimar in the adjacent *département* of La Drôme. As we drew near, colourful home-made notices announcing today's Herb Fair fluttered from sign posts and roadside trees. I adore these small local events, usually organized by the *mairie* and a handful of dedicated villagers, often aided with an encouraging grant from the regional council.

Entering the village, we drove past a small glass and metal building that housed a producer of plant essences, and further on an artisanal unit for drying wild herbs of the *garrigue*. An open-air herb fair was a natural choice for this community. It would boost the local economy and attract visitors.

We parked the car in a large meadow and followed the throng of people through the narrow streets to the centre of the village. Even without the directional arrows, we were guided by the

seductive scents of the herbs and the drumbeat of the band in the square.

Market stalls had been arranged down one side of the street, each displaying herbs in some manner. Sturdy potted plants had been brought by specialist nurserymen from the surrounding region. A herb grower from Romans had an impressive and enticing range of rosemary and lavender. The next stall was simply a small garden table covered with newspaper and a display of plastic yoghurt pots holding rooted cuttings with modest, home-made labels explaining how to care for them. I found a plant I didn't recognize. It was liquorice, *réglisse*, and I popped it into my shopping basket while the stallholder advised me that the herb needed a cool, damp site.

Just as I was chatting to another local grower about the virtues of a large-leaved variety of the culinary sage, *Salvia* 'Bergattern', the strains of the brass band grew louder and we turned to see a procession of about thirty children walking and skipping along the street into the centre of the village. Dressed in green with flowers and herbs entwined in their hair, or woven into garlands encircling each tiny waist or neck, it was a medieval scene: young people celebrating the arrival of summer with dancing and gaiety. Man once relied upon such rituals as an invocation of fertility. Nowadays, sad to say, gardeners too often resort to the indiscriminate use of chemicals to perform the same function.

Further on, in the car park behind the *mairie*, a small mobile distillery had been set in place. It was about to start up, fired by bundles of dry wood burning brightly below the copper alembic that would extract the essential oils of lavender, thyme and other local herbs.

At the crossroads in the centre of the village, the *auberge* had established another outdoor woodfire, and above it was perched a vast metal paella dish in which rice, stained saffron yellow, bubbled and frothed. We immediately reserved a table for lunch and set off to explore the remaining attractions.

A stone barn was devoted to books on herbs including French editions of two of my own. I smiled on seeing that one of them, *Recipes from a French Herb Garden*, though written a decade earlier was now rather timely. I began to fill the corners of my shopping basket with bars of herb-scented soap, bottles of essential oils and packets of dried herbs to take to England.

In no time, it seemed, the *apéritif* hour had arrived and stallholders began to cover their displays of goods before disappearing in the direction of the local cafés. We walked back to the *auberge* and took our appointed places for lunch.

Some time later – I have a hazy memory that the church clock was striking four – we departed from Le Puy Saint Martin, replete in every sense, the car and ourselves fragrant with fresh and dried herbs as we drove contentedly home.

CHAPTER TEN

June

In almost every town and village across the south of France, on market stalls and in grocery shops, you can find doll-size sacks of *herbes de Provence* for sale. These small bags, made from gaily coloured Provençal prints, or coarse brown hessian, contain a highly aromatic blend of dried herbs from the *garrigue,* the desolate limestone upland of the Midi.

Of the many *aromates* used in French cooking, none proclaims its provenance so intensely, none evokes a place, a climate and the sheer glory of summer living with such vigour. For *herbes de Provence* represent the quintessential flavour of a region, an actual *goût de terroir.*

It is usual, here, to find differing opinions on the composition of true *herbes de Provence.* Some say five herbs are necessary, others argue for eight, or even twelve different plants. All agree, though, on the crucial four: thyme, sage, rosemary and marjoram and these are the herbs whose flavours dominate the *mélange.* That said, many variations exist. Over the years I have come across packets of *herbes de Provence* which contain fennel, basil, mint, finely broken bay leaves and even crushed lavender. Like Provence itself, one warms to particular notes in this distinctive mixture – those that impart most pleasure.

Oddly enough in a land where freshness in ingredients is hallowed, *herbes de Provence* is normally composed of dried plants, carefully sorted and broken into small pieces about the size of a leaf of wild thyme or *serpolet*. Drying the herbs before blending intensifies their aroma, making them useful in the kitchen for the whole year.

Nevertheless, *herbes de Provence* are not for the faint-hearted: the flavour is robust and assertive, it speaks of the tastes of the Mediterranean, fully developed and irresistible. And although nervous cooks may add just a pinch to a light sauce, say, to introduce a hint of the south, in its homeland *herbes de Provence* are used with abandon, especially outdoors. A small handful or *poignée* is strewn over a leg of lamb or a whole large fish as it sits on a grid over a charcoal fire. The herbs might even be scattered over the embers themselves to perfume the air, or to aromatize grilled vegetables, or chunks of toasted country bread drizzled with olive oil.

In my kitchen, I keep some *herbes de Provence* in a lidded jar for winter use, but during the summer months a smooth wooden bowl holds the fragrant mixture beside the hob so that I can easily dip in my fingers. Hardly a day passes without some dish being flavoured with this appetizing potpourri.

HOWEVER ATTRACTIVE the little fabric bags of dried *herbes de Provence*, quite the best and most vibrant way of using these herbs is to grow them yourself, so that your cooking is enhanced by the more subtle flavours of the freshly picked version. Moreover, by selecting and picking the herbs, one can compose

an individual blend of *herbes de Provence*. There are, for instance, times when sage and thyme are all that is required to season a loin of pork for roasting; or when sprigs of that lovely trio of fresh fennel, mint and marjoram, tucked into the body of a freshly caught fish before cooking, will complement its flavour superbly.

Although in Saint Montan I have interpreted *herbes de Provence* fairly widely by planting as many native herbs of the region as possible, an appealing idea for a small domestic herb garden would be to plant just the culinary herbs of the Midi that are the most aromatic when growing.

A diminutive herb garden, or even a wide window box planted with the principal *herbes de Provence* would include rosemary, sage, wild thyme, marjoram, basil, fennel and mint. These are the major herbal flavours of Mediterranean summer cooking, offering satisfying variety to the most fastidious of cooks. And because all except the basil are perennial plants, the magnificent seven would provide culinary and aromatic pleasure for several years. Of course, if you have more room, then planting extra cultivars of each herb will unquestionably enhance your enjoyment.

BY MID-JUNE I WAS WEEDING the long narrow terrace again. Was this the third or fourth time I'd gone over this ground in as many months? To begin with, it is fascinating to see what plants appear from freshly tilled earth following decades of neglect. On the whole the seedlings were those of annual weeds, but sometimes edible evidence of the *curé's* appetite reappeared in the bright green spears of baby spinach or lettuce. More commonly, the blue-grey leaves of the wild onion, or jaunty seedlings of Swiss chard emerged with its bold white stems – known hereabouts as *blettes*. I leave the vegetable seedlings to grow to full-size, glad of all homegrown greenstuff for the table. But the weeds are another matter. They are relegated to my compost heap.

In an English garden I would have planted the upper terrace as a herbaceous border, but that would be out of place here. Back in September, when I had planned the garden, I had thought that the central strip of ground running the length of the narrow terrace would become a path from which one could tend the climbing plants on one side and the lavender and nepeta on the other. By now I was beginning to doubt the wisdom of this.

Pausing from my task, I looked around at the hillsides and noticing the high paths of scree, I realized that they were weed free. Suddenly I saw that there was a lesson in this. Why not make a scree bed on this long narrow terrace, with plants growing in pockets made in the covering of gravel or small stone chippings? A gravel terrace in the garden would not only be harmonious with the surrounding terrain but would conserve moisture in the ground and, at the same time, deal with the everlasting weed problem. I remember that John Brookes, one of the most sympathetic of garden designers, advises that 'a gravel bed is almost maintenance free'. *Parfait.*

The thought is the woman. I dropped everything and sped across to the loft over the garage where I'd thrown the old sheets of black plastic that had been splendid weed suppressors when I first began to clear the ground. Unrolling it on the raised terrace I saw that it would have to be cut to shape so that it ran the total length of thirty metres (nearly one hundred feet). In width, it needed to stretch from the foot of the dry-stone wall – leaving enough open ground for the climbing roses and honeysuckles to flourish – across the tiresomely weedy terrain to the row of lavender plants along the edge.

A recent news bulletin from the *mairie* had mentioned the admirably low expense incurred by me in making what was now officially recognized as the Saint Montan *jardin botanique*. The princely sum of 0.00 francs was quoted. The cost of the new gravel bed would not furrow the brow of Monsieur le Maire: I was happy to donate this vintage black plastic that had given such sterling service to the garden, and the stone chippings to cover it would be *gratuit* – they would come straight from the scree on the hillside.

FIRST I HAD TO REMOVE any perennial weeds from the area that was to become the gravel bed. It's extraordinary how persistent a deep-rooted wild clematis, or bramble bush – my particular *bête noire* – can be. On the one hand, one has to admire such determination. We know that a weed is only a plant in the wrong place but, unless carefully controlled, these pesky characters can plague your life in the garden. And having to extract them later, from under a sheet of plastic covered by a layer of gravel, is distinctly tedious. Small annual weeds, however, can be left to rot down under the impermeable mantle.

You need a still day to lay black plastic: a gust of wind just as you've spread out the stuff ruffles the surface, stretches your patience to breaking point, and can even gift-wrap you into the bargain. Luckily, where I was working was well protected from the breeze. And cutting the material is no problem. Sharp kitchen scissors slide through most grades of black plastic pretty efficiently, otherwise an army penknife is, as ever, invaluable.

Obtaining the scree or stone chippings was not difficult, just slow. Because they had to be fetched from the steep hillside above the herb garden, a bucketful at a time, it took some days to cover the plastic with an even layer. Eventually the job was done, and the effect was pleasing. The new surface of limestone chippings supplied another texture in the garden and light was reflected off the pale, crushed rocks, which in a shady, north-facing border is a useful attribute.

The most exciting aspect of the new gravel bed was that I had, in effect, extended the garden. So, joy of joys, I now had more ground in which to plant. In my own garden I still had an assortment of small shrubs and perennials growing in pots awaiting their ideal home. I had transplanted a seedling juniper found under one of my olive trees, and there were some digitalis plants that I'd sown in early spring which needed to be moved to permanent quarters. Some pots contained rooted cuttings brought from friends' gardens – one of the nicest ways of extending one's own. In fact, one of the best Devon gardeners I know created her large and lovely garden entirely from cuttings from elsewhere. These usually came from friends' gardens, though she had also developed an amazing sleight of hand involving a dropped handkerchief for procuring a shoot of a particularly desirable plant spotted growing in a public place!

With a selection of the potted plants in my battered old wheelbarrow I returned to the herb garden. I arranged the pots on the gravel, and in each place I swept aside some of the chippings and cut a hole in the plastic wide enough to scoop out some earth. After mixing a handful of compost into the bottom of the hole, each plant was inserted, leaving a narrow margin of bare earth around each one for catching rainwater.

Depending on your taste in gardening, a gravel bed can be planted with low-growing herbs that enjoy rock garden conditions including ajugas, purslane, stonecrop and houseleeks. Indeed, such is the interest in this kind of gardening that there is now a wide choice of suitable small plants. In the herb garden gravel bed, which was on a slightly raised terrace and backed by

the stone wall, taller plants and herbs were called for. Here was the ideal place for the statuesque cardoon, whose large, thistle-like flowers of late summer look like big blue powder puffs. A seedling of Himalayan honeysuckle, *Leycesteria Formosa* (also known as the nutmeg tree in my part of Devon) would do well here, with plenty of room for the long curving stems with their arresting purple-red bracts and shiny black berries. Now I had space for a pineapple tree, *Cytisus Battandieri*, and for even more of my beloved buddleias – the magnificent 'Black Knight' would look handsome against the grey limestone. Planting up a gravel bed takes remarkably little time – it is perfect for those impatient people who actually enjoy what has now been dubbed 'instant gardening'.

THE SUMMER SOLSTICE, when the sun moves into a lower orbit, occurs on or around the feast of St Jean. The day has long been a high point in the summer calendar of the Midi. In the past, huge fires were lit on midsummer's eve to celebrate the longest day; in Valréas in Vaucluse, a torchlit procession marks the five-hundred-year-old tradition of le Petit St-Jean with the coronation of a young boy from the town. From the earliest times, midsummer day has been marked by revelry and rites in many parts of the northern hemisphere.

The day was once regarded as the most auspicious time to collect the medicinal and culinary herbs known as the *herbes de la Saint-Jean* which were dried for use in the year ahead. In the beautiful arcaded Place aux Herbes, in Uzès, the annual Garlic Fair is held on the feast of St Jean, when the new season's crop of the 'stinking rose' is offered for sale.

The hottest weeks of the summer are about to begin, and rain is so unlikely and unwelcome that an old Saint Montan rhyme says: *Rain and cold on the day of St Jean means little wine and less grain.*

Within days, as the temperature climbs, the most characteristic sound of the Midi summer can be heard: the mating song of the cicada or *cigale*. These black and yellow winged insects feed on the sap of plants, but it is not until the extreme heat of late June or early July that the male cicada reveals his presence with an insistent call, produced by a sound box at the base of his abdomen. Fossil remains show that cicadas existed in the Ardèche eight million years ago. Today there are fifteen different species of this remarkable insect that stays below ground for most of its life, emerging in adult form during high summer to live for only a few more months. The chant of the cicada disappears quite suddenly one day in September when the heat of summer is at an end.

Few people have seen a cicada, yet its image is used widely as decoration here. It appears on paper and fabrics and scores of labels for jars and bottles – you even see enormous, glazed ceramic cicadas fixed high up on the outside walls of houses. This shy creature is not only the harbinger of high summer – it is also considered a portent of good luck.

Chapter Eleven

July

SOMETIMES, early on a July morning, the village is blissfully quiet. The stream is mute, trickling slowly over the stones, in places disappearing from view to emerge in a small pool where dragonflies swoop low.

A slight zephyr descends from the gorge, rustling the leaves on the poplar and lime trees as it makes its way through the village towards the funnelling valley of the Rhône. Then the breeze drops, and you have to strain your ears to catch any noise at all.

A bee arrives to collect nectar from the rosemary flowers. I hear the distinctive screech of my neighbour Monsieur Reynaud's metal gate as he sets off to the village for his daily baguettes. Then the church clock strikes the hour. After three minutes it will strike again so that no one is any doubt about the time.

The drone of a two-stroke *motobécane* making its sinous way down the hairpin road from Larnas can be heard. In a moment or two it passes the herb garden, the driver waving his arm. A tractor rumbles by and, even though absorbed in my task, I can tell it is July as a few seconds later a cloud of lavender scent floods the garden. I look up and see Farmer Guérin's trailer piled high with the soft grey stalks, making its way up the gorge in bottom gear. Now that the old distillery in the valley has closed, the harvested lavender is taken up to the new plant on the plateau.

Distilling lavender oil is basically a simple process. Bundles of freshly cut lavender are squashed into a tall iron cylinder and heated over a wood fire. Seen across the fields on a dark night, a working distillery with its huge flames raging around the sides of the vast black drum looks like a scene from Lucifer's kitchen. As the water in the drum beneath the lavender boils, the steam releases the essential oil of lavender from the blue-grey seeds. The distilled liquid is run off, then trickled over pipes of refrigerant until cold enough for the mixture to separate into water at the base of the chamber with the layer of essential oil floating on top. Then the oil is decanted into containers leaving the water behind.

Lavender farmers collect the oil from the distillery, in proportion to the size of their delivery. Growers then sell the oil themselves or to other lavender oil purveyors. There is a price difference between essence of true lavender and extract of lavandin. And, reasonably enough, the further from the point of production that you buy the oil, the higher the price. Monsieur Guérin grows so much lavender he sells some of the oil to bottlers in distant *départements* where it is doubtless sold at twice and three times the price we pay at his farm gate.

Madame Guérin sells some of the lavender essence from an old cupboard in the farmyard. Each September I buy enough new season's oil to last all year. We sprinkle it in hot baths, in drawers of clothes and around the house – though I use the cheaper lavandin extract for sprinkling on rugs and cushions as a moth deterrent. It is rare to have a day when the house is not scented with this wonderful fragrance. I rub lavender oil on to my wrists, elbows, and knees, to keep mosquitoes and other flying insects at bay. Madame Guérin usually tucks into my basket one of her blue paper lists giving many of the old-fashioned uses for lavender oil, for it is an antiseptic and can even be applied to minor cuts and grazes. In the past, lavender oil was one of the most important medicaments for country people – a friend still adds a few drops to a cube of sugar for sucking slowly to sooth a cough – and many are understandably reluctant to abandon it for expensive chemical alternatives.

Due to the heat in July, few gardeners – and certainly not this fair-skinned English one – can work outdoors beyond ten o'clock in the morning, or resume gardening until late afternoon. Fortunately there is normally less work to do at this time of year, beyond dead-heading and trimming, and irrigation where necessary, after sunset.

So this is the time of year when a gardener can relax by visiting others' gardens. I like to pack a picnic and drive over the Rhône at Viviers to visit two of my favourite, more established, herb gardens.

At Garde Adhémar, perched on the hillside looking down over the flat valley of the Rhône, is a large formal herb garden that I've watched develop from its straggly beginnings fifteen years ago. The garden is now a splendid sight, particularly from

the observation platform against the parapet above it. In midsummer, the garden's wide sun-ray pattern of long narrow beds is planted with yellow, orange and red blooms, a neat horticultural reflection of the setting sun opposite as it sinks towards the horizon of the Cévennes. The beds are edged with traditional low-clipped box hedges and the herb garden spreads over several levels with narrow paths of fine sand. There is an attractive metal pergola of old roses and the encircling wooden arches that have been recently erected to provide some protection from the Mistral are gradually softening with climbing plants.

A thirty-minute drive through purple fields of lavandin and rolling vineyards brings you to Nyons, famed for its olives and its fine oil. Lying in a cleft in the Baronnies, Nyons benefits from its own micro-climate; one November we drove to Nyons through a snow storm to buy freshly pressed olive oil, and found that the surrounding countryside and hills lay under a thick white blanket while in Nyons itself the mimosa was about to bloom and palm trees flourished in the gardens.

Downstream from the high-hooped Roman bridge in Nyons lies the '*Jardin des Arômes*' in a charming site among oak trees on the Promenade de la Digue. Created in 1983, this herb garden of two hundred species of aromatic plants is informal and natural in design. Irregularly shaped beds of mixed planting – sage jostles with scented roses, rosemary sits beside santolinas – are arranged around meandering paths which are sometimes paved, sometimes gravelled. A copper alembic once used for distilling essential oils has been placed like a modern sculpture in the centre of one bed. Stone seats are hidden in shady corners, each a welcome retreat in which to pause for a few moments to enjoy the scents of the plants and watch the river tumbling past.

Like every gardener inspired by another's efforts, I returned fizzing with fresh ideas and resolutions. In the Nyons garden I discovered a tree I didn't know, a *Melia azedarach*, the Bead Tree, or Persian Lilac, described in the essential Royal Horticultural Society encyclopedia as 'Deciduous, spreading tree. Has dark green leaves with many leaflets and fragrant, star-shaped pinkish-lilac flowers in spring, followed by pale orange-yellow fruits in autumn.' I added the name to my list of small trees suitable for a herb garden.

WHILE IN THE Garde Adhémar garden, I had been smitten by the clear-pink perfumed rose, 'Comte de Chambord'. This long-flowering Portland Damask from 1863 has attractive grey-green foliage and a camellia-like bloom, and can even be grown in a container – perfect for an aromatic garden.

On our return journey we had stopped at a garden centre and I had been tempted by an acceptably convincing reproduction of a medieval stone urn – simple enough in design to go well in the Saint Montan garden. I planned to fill it with scented-leaf geraniums, one of the finest potted plants for a herb garden, especially when placed waist-high where the fragrance can be easily appreciated. Though their flowers are modest they are not unappealing, but the real joy of these plants is the intense perfume they produce in their leaves. French *parfumeurs* distil the essence from the well-known rose-scented geranium, *Pelargonium graveolens*. Other attractive varieties include the small-leaved *P. crispum* with its orange fragrance, and the lemon-rose scented *P. radens* with its filigree-like foliage.

No collection of scented-leaved geraniums should omit the handsome *P. quercifolium*, whose large, felty leaves are splashed with bronze, and I have a special fondness for the cultivar, 'Lady Plymouth', with its pretty variegated leaves. Like all geraniums and pelargoniums, scented-leaf varieties are not frost-hardy, so they should be moved under cover during the winter, either into

a warm porch or conservatory or, as favoured by the Victorians, into the house so that they continue to give pleasure, perfuming the air whenever their leaves are touched.

If you prefer to fill large pots or a *jardinière* for a herb garden with hardy plants – subjects that would not require moving under cover each winter – then blue or white agapanthus take some beating, or more unusual varieties of the woody-stemmed Mediterranean plants such as rosemary and lavender which work well especially if accompanied by a small-leaved thyme or marjoram. More seasonal, but more fragrant, are lilies, especially the Easter lily, and carnations.

ALL WEEK THE VILLAGE had been preparing for its medieval fête: canvas banners had been hoisted into place above the road at all entrances. Immense pine columns had been delivered to the parking area on the road just above the herb garden. Then the work crew or *gens de technique* from the *mairie* arrived with teams of scouts (recruited from all over France to help Les Amis de Saint Montan restore the medieval buildings) for the next stage in the proceedings.

Each wooden pole was loaded on to a tractor, making it look like a motorized medieval knight armed with a tournament lance. Then Roland Reynaud drove the machine carefully up the steep slope to the Portalet gateway into the old village. Here the poles were carried up to the château by groups of cheerful, singing scouts to the point where M. Wyss supervised a reconstruction of the medieval scaffolding used in its building five centuries earlier. In the village square, stalls were assembled, and there was an air of excitement as small children ran through the narrow cobbled streets to show off their medieval-style outfits.

The fête day dawned to perfect July weather. Without a cloud in the sky, the sun warmed the air even in the cool, shaded alleys of the old village. At midday the sound of horses' hooves echoed from the stone buildings as a procession of villagers dressed in period costume made its way out of the village square. It came slowly past the herb garden on its way to the San Samonta chapel. Here, the first part of an historical drama, written specially for the occasion and based on a tale of disputed inheritance, was played to an audience of villagers and visitors, and even if few could follow the intricacies of the plot, the atmosphere of merriment was infectious. After fifteen minutes the procession returned from the chapel to the village centre – in good time for a cool glass of *pastis* before lunch.

During the afternoon there were more diversions: stilt walkers disguised as satyrs amused passers-by but sometimes terrified small children with their antics; a normally respectable villager, dressed in rags, ran amok as a mad woman muttering gibberish, to everyone's delight. The market stalls opened for business, selling medieval-inspired artefacts such as studded leather purses, polished stones and hand-woven cloth. There was even a stall with delicious pies made to a sixteenth-century recipe. And a wandering band of minstrels played medieval music on pipes and crumhorns. Everyone enjoyed this re-enactment of a day in the life of the village five centuries earlier.

Even the village herb garden benefited from the medieval fête: the next day some of the scouts delivered a few dustbin bags of *crottins des chevaux* – horse droppings – cleared from the streets. A first-rate fertilizer for the climbing roses!

Chapter Twelve

August

Aᴜɢᴜsᴛ ɪs ᴡᴇʟʟ ᴇsᴛᴀʙʟɪsʜᴇᴅ as *the* holiday month in France. Not only are the French themselves *en vacances* – it is notoriously futile to seek a response from officialdom at this time – but most of the tourists from abroad are here, too.

Now that Saint Montan has become a *village de caractère* – in the Ardèche, a designation reserved for places distinguished by their age and beauty, and with fewer than one thousand inhabitants – there are many more visitors, some of whom have consulted the *mairie's* new website. Discovering medieval villages on the Internet is a nice kind of anachronism.

Ever since I had begun to cultivate the herb garden, there had been a lot of interest from villagers and passers-by. Its location meant that I could not garden secretly – there is no hiding place. This public garden is constantly on public view, which is, of course, an asset for a community garden. Consequently, many of the plants in the garden were donated by villagers who, on seeing freshly tilled earth, brought me rooted cuttings and small seedlings from their own gardens. One might even say that the herb garden represents a horticultural roll of honour of those villagers who contributed in a practical way. And the planting itself amounts to a valuable historical record of varieties that have been grown in the locality, usually for generations, sometimes even for centuries.

One of the obligations of a French *village de caractère* is that organized tours be available for visitors. Carole Naimo, events organizer at the *mairie*, has recruited several knowledgeable local people to conduct, at appointed times, walking tours of the village; these take in the fortified château, the medieval streets and restored houses, the site of the sixteenth-century *hôpital* and the disused grain and olive mills.

On their way to the chapel of San Samonta and the *source de fièvres*, visitors pass the herb garden. While I have been constructing it, some people have paused to look, some to ask about it, and the keenest cross to the apex of the little stone bridge. A few gardening devotees enter the garden itself, and walk along the narrow paths to inspect the plants, though they rarely interrupt my work since the French are notably polite and considerate.

WHILE MOST PRIVATE GARDENS do not boast plant labels, they are found in gardens large enough to be open to the public, or in those owned by plantsmen with collections of rare specimens. But a public garden that has many visitors with varying degrees of knowledge should display plant labels; they not only inform but often educate, for there is pleasure in sharing with others a knowledge of plants.

It had always been my plan to have name plates for each plant in the herb garden. Reasonably enough this was not an early priority. But now that most of the planting was complete, and many more people were visiting the garden, I clearly needed to identify the plants.

I already had my supply of name plates. Some months earlier, having realized that French garden centres could only offer garish yellow plastic labels, I had scanned the advertizements in gardening journals from France and North America. I was looking for a style that resembled old-fashioned lead name plates like the 'Acme' ones of my youth – plates that were subdued in colour and shape yet answered their purpose without being distracting. I discovered some good-looking name plates made in America, but the cost of mailing them was prohibitive, so I had finally consulted my friend Julie Toll, the garden designer, whose taste in plant labels I knew I could trust. Luckily, at that time, she was looking for the same kind of thing for a large garden she had designed in the Caribbean. She faxed back details of an excellent style and she placed an order for me. We handed over the bag of metal labels at the Chelsea Flower Show, and after touring the ever-inspiring display gardens with Julie, I caught the Eurostar train back to Saint Montan. The tags had been sitting in my garden store ever since. Now was the time to inscribe them.

I had been studying plant labels for months, and decided that those at the fine botanic garden in Lyons should be my model. Fortunately I had taken notes and photographs and so one hot morning I sat on the shady terrace in my own garden and began to follow the instructions given for marking the plates. Having made a mess of my first attempt, I realized that it is essential to write out on paper exactly what you want on the name plate *before* starting. Embossed labels cannot be rewritten.

After a bit of practice I got the hang of how to position the label in the guide and then hammer the letters on to it. At the end of the morning I had a clutch of name plates waiting to be put in place. Using a small rubber hammer, I tapped them into the dry earth in front of each plant. Now, at last, the village herb garden quite definitely took on the appearance of the promised *jardin botanique* of Saint Montan.

HALFWAY THROUGH THE MONTH, the summer is unquestionably in decline. As early as the tenth day of August there is, for the first time, the merest hint of autumn in the air. In the herb garden I notice the morning shadows are longer and one's eyes and skin detect that the sun has lost its ferocity.

As a result, the season is lovely, the scents are stronger, the greens and blues of the shade are deeper. This is a perfect time for the gardener, the painter or photographer, when the glaring knife-sharp contrast between sun and shade of high summer has subtly moderated. Of course, the luminosity is still far greater than in Britain and the rest of northern Europe, and I remember that when our children were young we always took our holidays in these lingering days of summer when the pace of life is gentler.

Now, once again, I'm able to garden for an hour or so after breakfast: loosening the soil from errant weeds, gently pruning shrubs back into shape to persuade them to put on one final spurt of growth that can be enjoyed during the warm quiet days of autumn.

My natural inclination is to allow plants to look after themselves and grow largely untended, so that their form and bearing are easily appreciated. Yet in a small garden one soon learns the virtues of grooming the plants by judicious trimming and pruning. In a Mediterranean climate this has other advantages, too. By cutting back some of the top growth of fleshy or leggy plants in late summer, transpiration is reduced, less watering is required, and the plants looks happier. And in any garden in the path of the Mistral, plants have to be well tethered, either with supports or by their own roots, to prevent windrock, so keeping top growth neat is to be recommended. I find that the most valuable garden tool in the garden during August is a pair of secateurs.

TOWARDS THE MIDDLE of the month, the day of the sun's final eclipse of the century arrives. Daybreak is bright and sunny with a gentle breeze. But by mid-morning the light begins to fade, losing some of its intensity, as if obscured by cloud. Yet the sky is still bright blue as the light grows curiously feeble and greyish, not the rich yellow of August. Looking at the sun through safety spectacles, it is clear that the luminous disc is occluded on one side.

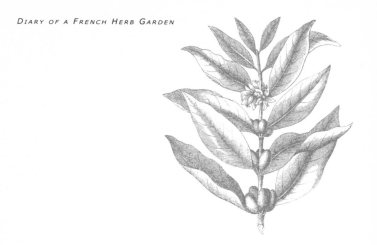

At noon we tune in to French television where cameras in Normandy are monitoring the total eclipse. Six hundred kilometres further south we are experiencing a partial eclipse but its effect is still astonishing. At the moment of total eclipse in the north, we have a mysterious and unusual daylight in the south – it is almost like immensely bright moonlight, rather as if the light of the sun is obscured by the smoke of a thousand fires. Were the final days of Pompeii like this? The sound of cheering from the television announces that the minute or so duration of total eclipse is over, and people's faces on the screen show both relief and astonishment, as if our planet had escaped a dreadful fate. As the daylight suddenly regains its vigour it is as if we'd been given back our sun.

The air temperature in August is still very high, the thermometer hovers around the mid-thirties Celsius. When one of the Parisian scouts arrives to help in the herb garden, he offers to weed the paths for a couple of hours. We give him cool drinks and an ice cream but what he would prefer, he says shyly, is a cold shower. Baden Powell would have been proud of him.

With so many people on holiday during August, life in Saint Montan is very social. Inevitably, there is a festive atmosphere. The village holds its annual *fête votive* with a small funfair and outdoor dancing. There is a flute concert in the San Samonta chapel, and one night a group of local rock climbers staged a fairly scary demonstration of tightrope walking and acrobatics high above the gorge – without a safety net!

This is the season of long, leisurely lunches under the fig tree and even longer late suppers on the terrace, with food grilled over charcoal and flat breads and butterflied lamb baked in our outdoor wood oven. If you're lucky at the end of the evening, when the candles are blown out, a few glow-worms lodged in the crevices of the dry-stone wall might put on their astonishing display of luminescence.

IN THE SOUTH OF FRANCE, this is the time of year for all dutiful gardeners to relax and enjoy the fruits of their labours. In her splendid *potager*, Jeannette Doize is picking basketfuls of the most superb vegetables which she generously distributes to her friends. One morning she arrives with a few seedlings of the mandrake plant, *Atropa mandragora* – one of this year's experiments. Mrs Grieve describes this legendary plant as the object of many strange superstitions. Yet Pliny wrote that the root was chewed for its anaesthetic properties, and even today the plant is used in homeopathy. The mature plant develops swollen and contorted roots and produces long, strap-like leaves. While hardly essential in a herb garden, the mandrake is a fascinating addition to the exotic island.

I HARVEST HERBS for drying: bundles of wild thyme and sage from our own hillside. From my own garden, I pick a bouquet of bay leaves, fennel, mint and lemon verbena for my daughter to take back to her London kitchen. And from the village herb garden there are small posies of fresh herbs, tied with narrow ribbon, to give as presents.

After so long without rain the seed heads on angelica, chives and bronze fennel are sufficiently dry to cut and save for next season. I place the seed heads, herb by herb, in separate paper bags and hang them in a dry place for eight weeks until the seeds can be shaken easily from their pods. Small envelopes of selected seeds will later be labelled and posted to gardening friends with their Christmas card; if we are to protect the cultural diversity of the planet we shall need to save and exchange seed far more than in the past.

Only gentle tasks are required in the herb garden – dead heading and tying straggly growths of roses and honeysuckle. The summer-flowering clematis are putting on a brilliant display. Few are lovelier than the large, white *C. Henryi*.

It is a good moment to take a few cuttings of your favourite pelargoniums so that they root well before the winter. And heeding advice from the estimable Miss Jekyll, every week or so there is a general post for my potted plants. Small tubs of lilies, a pot of purple-flowering solanum, or another of mauve and white lantana in full bloom, are sunk into the ground where they look their best and add interest to the garden during this last lazy month of summer.

Epilogue

The Second September

I write on the ninth day of the ninth month of the ninety-ninth year of the century.

We have the village to ourselves again, and the tranquillity feels almost physical. The leaves on the poplar quiver in the light breeze, they shimmer like a thousand facets, first pale then dark. Water from the *source de fièvres* trickles over the large stones in the bed of the river.

At the stream's narrowest point, visiting children have moved some big stones to form a diminutive bridge. Heavy autumn rain will sweep their construction down to the centre of the village where the water course meets the larger wider *ruisseau d'Ellieux*, a river once so important in the village that it could drive two grain mills. In medieval times, when the water table was several metres higher, the Ellieux river was crossed with a drawbridge which gave entry to the ancient fortified village.

A fluttering in the big almond tree attracts my attention and I detect a couple of wrens, hopping playfully from twig to twig. In France, the wren is known by its cumbrous Latin name, *troglodyte*. But just seeing this tiny, shy bird feels like a blessing, and finding them in your garden is said by gardeners to bring good fortune. Then I hear the cry of a jay, the brightly hued watchman of the forest. I look up and see, silhouetted against the azure sky, above the gap in the hills known as *le trou de madame*, an unbelievable sight. An eagle glides slowly across the gorge, majestically riding the thermal like a king come to claim his land.

An eagle in flight is unforgettably beautiful, the vast wing span which governs its slow silent passage making it truly the most imperial of birds. After a minute or so he is joined by his mate, and they circle slowly to the south, rising to the level of the plateau, then head towards the dense forest on its flank. For a moment I stand transfixed, then I realize that something has happened that is cause for quiet celebration: at long last, after an absence of generations, the eagle of the Mediterranean known as Bonelli's Eagle, may have returned to the *val chaud*.

By MID-MORNING M. Reynaud is watering the tall 'Peace' roses and bright red dahlias in his wife's flower garden. The summer is not yet over, the drought still reigns. Though the night temperature has fallen, I still need to irrigate the garden every evening, just to keep plants alive. During the winter, I hope the *mairie* will install a proper automatic watering system.

Patrolling the garden at the end of each day, directing the waterspray to plants that need it most, brings home to me the gulf between gardening in southern France and southern England. It is true that, once established here, plants grow at a prodigious rate compared with northern lands, but getting plants established is far more difficult. How easy it was to heel in a seedling or even take a softwood cutting, straight into the loam of my Devon garden! Small wonder that England's mild, damp climate accommodates some of the finest gardens in the world. Had Napoleon actually reached English shores he would have discovered, not a nation of shopkeepers, but a land of gardeners. Yet, even given this horticultural heritage, I have found gardening south of 45 degrees latitude more challenging and exciting than I'd ever envisaged. It has been a true voyage of discovery.

IN OTHER SEPTEMBERS the rain would have arrived by now, the dusty earth would have been doused, surplus water would have cascaded over the bare rocks and overnight the spring at the foot of the Grotte de Lourdes would have begun to trickle over the sadly dessicated ground.

I stroll out of the garden, over the stone bridge, and turn upstream to follow the course of the river, stepping on the large

boulders that form a crossing. The sound of chattering water draws me to the *source de fièvres,* the everlasting spring that issues from the vertical face of the rock on the far side of the stream. The source feeds into a clear, deep pool where early autumn leaves are floating. As each dry leaf absorbs the water it sinks slowly to the bottom of the pool but then the current from the spring sends it up to the surface again. The leaf absorbs more water and descends once more, only to re-emerge into the air a minute later. Gazing at this seasonal version of perpetual motion is hypnotic and I stir from my reverie only as I become aware of the heat of the sun filtering through the branches of the lime tree overhead.

For the sun still provides ample heat for vegetation to grow, and towards the end of the morning it is too hot to garden out of the shade. I take refuge on the terrace overlooking the garden, where we sit with a cool bottle of local rosé wine and some black olives. I never tire of gazing at the view, the subtly changing flora, the outline of the shrubs and trees against the remorselessly cerulean sky, the ochre and grey rocks that change so imperceptibly that they appear as constant and comforting companions.

The scents from the garden even reach us on the terrace; they are more intense than in mid-summer, the slightly cooler days with a hint of dew at night make the essential oils aromatize for longer. But it is not just the herbs that scent the air, the leaves from the lime trees and the *micocoulier* – said to be the legendary lotus tree of the ancients whose fruit induced a state of ambrosial bliss – also add their perfume. Even more insistent is the delicious wild acacia whose dry leaves still surrender their enchanting scent.

On 15 September the rain arrives. At first it is a light baptism, so I leave the hose pipe on the ground. But the next day serious rainfall begins. I coil up my trusty and much-used watering system. The major work of the garden is over. I begin to write this account.

'The desire, the capacity to enjoy, is an instinct,' wrote Dean Hole, the nineteenth-century cleric and gardening writer, 'the love of flowers is innate, a remembrance of Eden.' He reminds us that all gardeners are simply custodians, each handing on the tradition of stewardship, of protecting the land and caring for the ground, until the next generation succeeds us.

That I am not the proprietor of this French herb garden matters not a jot. Indeed, this aspect has enhanced my joy. Working here has not been solely self-gratifying, it has also been a shared pleasure, carried out for others with a result that, I hope, will survive for some time. Creating this garden has been inspired by gratitude for the happiness that France has always given me. My work has been, quite simply, a labour of love.

Diary of a
French Herb
Garden

Diary of a French Herb Garden Plant List

CHAPTER THREE: NOVEMBER

CHAPTER FOUR: DECEMBER

CHAPTER FIVE: JANUARY

CHAPTER SIX: FEBRUARY

CHAPTER SEVEN: MARCH

Chapter Eight: April

CHAPTER ELEVEN: JULY

CHAPTER TWELVE: AUGUST

EPILOGUE: SECOND SEPTEMBER

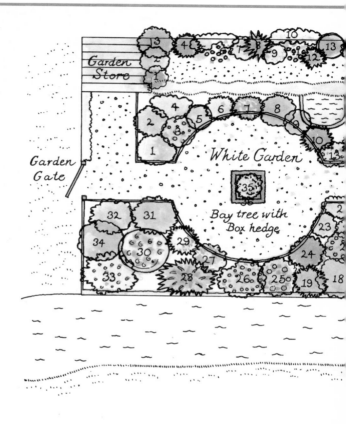

PLANTING PLAN OF THE
FRENCH HERB GARDEN AT
SAINT MONTAN

(LEFT-HAND SIDE)

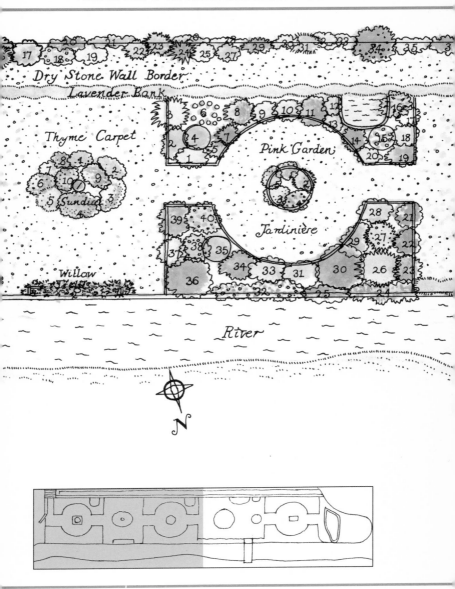

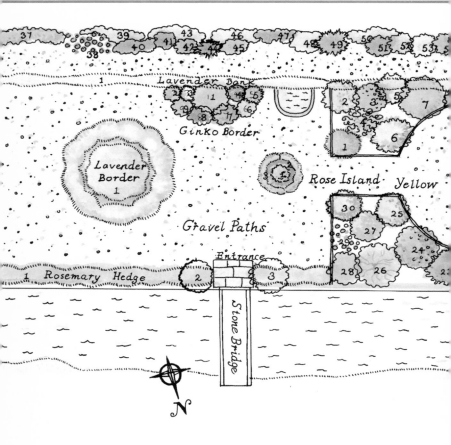

PLANTING PLAN OF THE
FRENCH HERB GARDEN AT
SAINT MONTAN
(RIGHT-HAND SIDE)

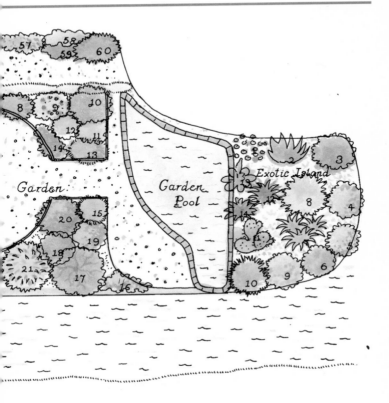

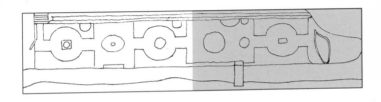

Planting Plan

Perennials and Biennials Only

DRY-STONE WALL BORDER – LEFT TO RIGHT

1. Micocoulier of Provence or Nettle tree, *Celtis australis*
2. Himalayan honeysuckle or False nutmeg, *Leycesteria Formosa*
3. Single purple lilac, *Syringa* 'Charles Joly'
4. Japanese anemone, *Anemone hupehensis*
5. Climbing rose, *Rosa* 'Wedding Day'
6. Canterbury bell, *Campanula medium* 'Bells of Holland'
7. Shrub rose, *Rosa* 'Penelope'
8. Cardoon, *Cynara cardunculus*
9. Sweet pea, *Lathyrus odoratus*
10. Clematis, *Clematis* 'Nelly Moser'
11. Canterbury bell, *Campanula medium* 'Bells of Holland'
12. Heuchera, *Heuchera* 'Palace Purple'
13. Shrub rose, *Rosa* 'Felicia'
14. Carpetting campanula, *Campanula portenschlagiana*
15. Honeysuckle, *Lonicera periclymenum* 'Serotina'
16. Petovskia, *Petovskia atriplicifolia* 'Blue Spire'
17. Shrub rose, *Rosa centifolia* 'Rose des Peintres'
18. Carpetting campanula, *Campanula portenschlagiana*

19. Shrub rose, *Rosa centifolia* 'The Bishop'
20. Summer jasmine or Jessamine, *Jasminum officinale*
21. Climbing rose, *Rosa* 'Polka'
22. Japanese anemone, *Anemone hupehensis*
23. Buddleia or Butterfly bush, *Buddleia davidii* 'Black Knight'
24. Foxglove, *Digitalis purpurea*
25. Lemon balm, *Melissa officinalis*
26. Climbing rose, *Rosa* 'Landora aka Sunblest'
27. Hellebore, *Helleborus foetidus*
28. Rambling rose, *Rosa* 'Dorothy Perkins'
29. Honeysuckle, *Lonicera periclymenum* 'Serotina'
30. Himalayan honeysuckle or False nutmeg, *Leycesteria Formosa*
31. Passion flower, *Passiflora caerulea*
32. Climbing rose, *Rosa* 'Alberic Barbier'
33. Honeysuckle, *Lonicera japonica* 'Halliana'
34. Fig tree, *Ficus carica*
35. Himalayan honeysuckle or False nutmeg, *Leycesteria Formosa*
36. Clematis, *Clematis* 'Henryi'
37. Passion flower, *Passiflora caerulea*
38. Globe artichoke, *Cynara cardunculus*
39. Climbing rose, *Rosa* 'Sutter's Gold'
40. Snow-in-summer, *Cerastium tomentosum*
41. Hardy geranium, *Geranium ibericum*
42. Aptenia, *Aptenia cordifolia*
43. Climbing rose, *Rosa* 'Albertine'
44. Dalmation bearded iris, *Iris pallida*
45. Heartsease or Wild pansy, *Viola tricolor*
46. Climbing rose, *Rosa* 'Little Rambler'
47. Honeysuckle, *Lonicera japonica* 'Halliana'

48. Coronilla, *Coronilla valentina*
49. Acanthus or Bear's breeches, *Acanthus mollis*
50. Himalayan honeysuckle or False nutmeg, *Leycesteria Formosa*
51. Single purple lilac, *Syringa* 'Charles Joly'
52. Hellebore, *Helleborus foetidus*
53. 'Bowles' mint, *Mentha rotundifolia* 'Bowles'
54. Feverfew, *Tanacetum parthenium* 'Aurea'
55. Yellow Banksian rose, *Rosa Banksiae lutea*
56. Hellebore, *Helleborus foetidus*
57. Summer jasmine or Jessamine, *Jasminum officinale*
58. Climbing rose, *Rosa* 'Rambling Rector'
59. Hibiscus, *Hibiscus* unkown seedling
60. Buddleia, *Buddleia alternifolia*

WHITE GARDEN

1. Lemon verbena, *Lippia citriodora*
2. Pittosporum, *Pittosporum triloba*
3. Bush rose, *Rosa* 'Poker'
4. White hyssop, *Hyssopus officinalis* 'Alba'
5. Paeony, *Paeonia* 'White Wings'
6. Marjoram, *Origanum vulgare*
7. Variegated sage, *Salvia officinalis* 'Icterina'
8. Lemon balm, *Melissa officinalis*
9. Feverfew, *Tanacetum parthenium* 'Aurea'
10. White-flowered rosemary, *Rosmarinus officinalis* 'Alba'
11. Rue, *Ruta graveolens*
12. Variegated sage, *Salvia officinalis* 'Tricolor'
13. Pink, *Dianthus* 'Mrs Sinkins'
14. Southernwood, *Artemisia abrotanum*

15. Roman camomile or Lawn camomile, *Chamaemelum nobile*
16. Hardy geranium, *Geranium renardii*
17. Elderflower, *Sambucus nigra*
18. Strawberry tree, *Arbutus unedo*
19. Bronze fennel, *Foeniculum vulgare* 'Purpurescens'
20. Bush rose, *Rosa* 'Virgo'
21. Snow-in-summer, *Cerastium tomentosum*
22. Gomphostigma, *Gomphostigma virginatum*
23. Perpetual candytuft, *Iberis sempervirens*
24. White horehound, *Marrubium vulgare*
25. Elderflower, *Sambucus nigra*
26. Climbing rose, *Rosa* 'Alberic Barbier'
27. Thyme, *Thymus serpyllum*
28. White buddleia, *Buddleia davidii* 'White Bouquet'
29. Butcher's broom, *Ruscus aculeatus*
30. Bush rose, *Rosa* 'Iceberg'
31. Wormwood, *Artemisia absinthium*
32. Winter savory, *Satureja montana*
33. Mock orange, *Philadelphus coronarius*
34. Micocoulier of Provence, or Nettle tree, *Celtis australis*

BAY TREE BOX

35. Sweet bay, *Laurus nobilis*
36. Box, *Buxus sempervirens*

THYME CARPET

1. Stonecrop, *Sedum acre*

2. Long-leaf thyme, *Thymus doefleri 'Bressingham Pink'*
3. Garden thyme, *Thymus vulgaris*
4. Alysum, *Alysum montanum*
5. Wild Provençal thyme, *Thymus serpyllum*
6. Corsican mint, *Mentha requienii*
7. Lemon thyme, *Thymus* x *citriodorus*
8. Woolly thyme, *Thymus pseudolanuginosus*
9. Golden marjoram, *Origanum vulgare* 'Aureum'
10. Caraway thyme, *Thymus herba-barona*

WILLOW TRELLIS

1. Weeping willow, *Salix alba* 'Tristis'
2. Grape vine, *Vitis* 'Brandt'

PINK GARDEN

1. Spirea, *Spirea japonica* 'Anthony Waterer'
2. Hardy geranium, *Geranium incanum*
3. Tamarisk, *Tamarix ramosissima*
4. Shrub rose, *Rosa* 'Perle de Panachées'
5. Red-leaved sorrel, *Rumex sanguineus*
6. Day lily, *Hemerocallis lilio-asphodelus*
7. Liquorice, *Glycyrrhiza glabra*
8. Himalayan honeysuckle or False nutmeg, *Leycesteria Formosa*
9. Pineapple sage, *Salvia rutilans*
10. Hardy geranium, *Geranium x oxonianum* 'Winscombe'
11. Hibiscus, *Hibiscus syriacus*
12. Mallow, *Malva sylvestris*

13. Eau de cologne mint, *Mentha x piperita citrata*
14. Soapwort, *Saponaria officinalis*
15. Shrub rose, *Rosa* 'Salet'
16. Buddleia or Butterfly bush, *Buddleia davidii* 'Empire Blue'
17. Blue hyssop, *Hyssopus officinalis*
18. Large-leaved sage, *Salvia officinalis* 'Bergattern'
19. Garden or Common sage, *Salvia officinalis*
20. Perilla, *Perilla frutescens*
21. Sage, *Salvia nemorosa* 'May Night'
22. Blue viola, *Viola elatior*
23. Veronica spicata or Spiked speedwell, *Veronica spicata*
24. Wisteria, *Wisteria sinensis*
25. Blue passion flower, *Passiflora caerulea*
26. Deep pink buddleia, *Buddleia davidii* 'Royal Red'
27. Sea holly, *Eryngium tripartitum*
28. Clary sage, *Salvia sclarea*
29. Red-flowered sage, *Salvia microphylla* var. *neurepia*
30. Self-sown apple seedling, variety unknown
31. Rock rose, *Cistus crispus*
32. Climbing rose, *Rosa* 'Etoile de Hollande'
33. Bergenia, *Bergenia cordifolia* 'Purpurea'
34. Lamb's tongue, *Stachys byzantina* syn *S. lanata*
35. Shrub rose, *Rosa* 'Cardinal Richelieu'
36. Almond tree, *Prunus dolcis* 'Roseoplena'
37. Pink-flowered hyssop, *Hyssopus officinalis* 'Rosa'
38. Sedum, *Sedum spectabile*
39. Purple-leaved sage, *Salvia officinalis* 'Purpurascens'
40. Red valerian, *Centranthus rubra*

JARDINIERE

Scented leaf pelargonium or scented-leaf geranium:
1. *Pelargonium crispum* 'Old Spice'
2. *Pelargonium quercifolium*
3. *Pelargonium x fragrans*
4. Erigeron, *Erigeron karvinskianus*
5. Plectranthus or Swedish ivy, *Plectranthus coleoides*

LAVENDER BANK

1. Lavandin or '*lavande bâtarde*'

LAVENDER BORDER

1. Maritime lavender, *Lavandula dentata*

ROSEMARY HEDGE

1. Wild Mediterranean rosemary, *Rosmarinus officinalis*
2. Chaste tree, *Vitex agnus-castus*
3. Pineapple tree or Moroccan broom, *Cytisus battandieri*

GINKO BORDER

1. Ginko tree, *Ginko biloba*
2. Rosemary, *Rosmarinus officinalis* 'Tuscan Blue'
3. Rosemary, *Rosmarinus officinalis* 'Corsican Blue'

4. Rosemary, *Rosmarinus officinalis* 'Corsican Blue'
5. Rosemary, *Rosmarinus officinalis* 'Tuscan Blue'
6. Catmint, *Nepeta* x *faassenii* 'Souvenir d'André Chaudon'
7. Catmint, *Nepeta* x *faassenii*
8. Catmint, *Nepeta* x *faassenii*
9. Catmint, *Nepeta* x *faassenii* 'Souvenir d'André Chaudon'

ROSE ISLAND

1. Half-standard rose, *Rosa* 'Madame du Barry'
2. English lavender, *Lavandula angustifolia* 'Hidcote'
3. Rosemary, *Romarinus officinalis*

YELLOW GARDEN

1. Santolina or Cotton lavender, *Santolina chamaecyparris*
2. Myrtle, *Myrtus communis*
3. Bush rose, *Rosa* 'Toulouse Lautrec'
4. Corkscrew hazel, *Corylus avellana* 'Contorta'
5. Witch hazel, *Hamamaelis mollis*
6. Achillea, *Achillea clypeolata*
7. Judas tree, *Cercis siliquastrum*
8. Curry plant, *Helichrysum angustifolium* curry plant
9. Bush rose, *Rosa* 'Princess Caroline of Monaco'
10. Mimosa, *Acacia dealbata*
11. Achillea, *Achillea clypeolata*
12. Tansy, *Tanacetum vulgare*
13. Santolina or Cotton lavender, *Santolina chamaecyparris*
14. Yellow pansy, *Viola gracilis*
15. Santolina or Cotton lavender, *Santolina chamaecyparris*

16. Honeysuckle, *Lonicera japonica* 'Italliana'
17. Olive tree, *Olea europaea*
18. Bush rose, *Rosa* 'Mrs Pierre S. du Pont'
19. Euryops, *Euryops pectinatus*
20. Jerusalem sage, *Phlomis fruticosa*
21. Buddleia yellow, *Buddleia davidii* 'Golden Sunset'
22. St John's wort, *Hypericum perforatum*
23. Senecio, *Senecio laxifolius*
24. Bush rose, *Rosa* 'Frederic Mistral'
25. Chrysanthemum or '*Marguerite d'automne*',
    Chrysanthemum haradjanii
26. Loquat or Japanese medlar, *Eriobotrya japonica*
27. Santolina, *Santolina pinnata* subsp. neopolitana
    'Sulphurea'
28. Spurge, *Euphorbia cyparissias*
29. Gazania, *Gazania uniflora* 'Sundance'
30. Santolina or Cotton lavender, *Santolina chamaecyparris*

IVY TUB

1. Wild or garden ivy, *Hedera helix*
2. Variegated ivy, *Hedera helix* 'Eva'

EXOTIC ISLAND

1. Evening primrose, *Oenothera erythrosepala*
2. Agave, *Agave americana*
3. Chilean laurel, *Laurus serrata*
4. Bignonia or Trumpets of Jericho, *Campsis* x *tagliabuana*
   'Mme Gallen'

5. Sweet bay, *Laurus nobilis*
6. Lopezia, *Lopezia coronata*
7. Yucca, *Yucca gloriosa*
8. Mahonia, *Mahonia aquifolia* 'Charity'
9. Coronilla, *Coronilla velentina*
10. Wild asparagus, *Asparagus officinalis*
11. Prickly pear, *Opunta vulgaris*
12. Lemon grass, *Cymbopogon citratus*
13. Great mullein or Aaron's rod, *Verbascum thrapsus*
14. Purslane or Portalacea, *Portulaca oleracea*